PRAISE FOR

ON POINT

"My good friend Del Harris has written a uniquely insightful book that shows the importance and power of influence. Drawing on his extensive resume as a successful basketball coach, Del gives every reader a simple four step system to understanding the strategic part each of us plays in shaping and being shaped by the relational teams in our lives. On Point *will equip every reader with the tools necessary to maximize their potential while simultaneously helping others to do the same."*

DR. TONY EVANS

PRESIDENT, THE URBAN ALTERNATIVE
SENIOR PASTOR, OAK CLIFF BIBLE FELLOWSHIP
CHAPLAIN, DALLAS MAVERICKS AN DALLAS COWBOYS

"The characteristics and mindset needed to be On Point *are clearly presented in my good friend Del Harris' book. His four-step system leads to better 'life' teams—at home, at work, or in your community."*

JOHN CALIPARI

HEAD BASKETBALL COACH, UNIVERSITY OF KENTUCKY

*"*On Point *is a must read for those who hope to understand and live life through meaningful relationships. It promises to be one of the most compelling, well-structured approaches to our roles as influencers in today's society. As a lifelong friend, and a member of one of Del Harris' championship teams, my life, my family's lives, and those lives in the community in which I reside have been enriched by the concepts he shares through this kindred, thoughtful message."*

AVIS STEWART

FORMER PLAYER
VP EARLHAM COLLEGE, IN

ON POINT

ON POINT

FOUR STEPS TO BETTER LIFE TEAMS

DEL HARRIS

Former NBA Coach of the Year

Published by Advantage, Charleston, South Carolina.
Member of Advantage Media Group.

ADVANTAGE is a registered trademark and the Advantage colophon is a trademark of Advantage Media Group, Inc.

Printed in the United States of America.

ISBN: 978-159932-340-4
LCCN: 2012944302

This publication is designed to provide accurate and authoritative information in regard to the subject matter covered. It is sold with the understanding that the publisher is not engaged in rendering legal, accounting, or other professional services. If legal advice or other expert assistance is required, the services of a competent professional person should be sought.

Advantage Media Group is proud to be a part of the Tree Neutral® program. Tree Neutral offsets the number of trees consumed in the production and printing of this book by taking proactive steps such as planting trees in direct proportion to the number of trees used to print books. To learn more about Tree Neutral, please visit www.treeneutral.com. To learn more about Advantage's commitment to being a responsible steward of the environment, please visit www.advantagefamily.com/green

Advantage Media Group is a leading publisher of business, motivation, and self-help authors. Do you have a manuscript or book idea that you would like to have considered for publication? Please visit www.advantagefamily.com or call 1.866.775.1696

*Dedicated with love to my family and extended family of friends—
those who have been on the same teams with me and those who have
stood by me over these many years in our various arenas of life.
Thanks to you all.*

ACKNOWLEDGEMENTS

The problem with the acknowledgements section is that there are always so many people that contribute directly and indirectly, that it is impossible to mention everyone. But I will start with Nancy Lieberman and Dr. Dusty Rubeck, president of Dallas Christian College, for asking me to speak at events for them where the seed of this book was planted. Added thanks to Dusty for allowing me to formulate a syllabus to teach at DCC on team building that helped the book to materialize, and to the thirty-six students who endured the class as I worked through the concepts presented in this book. Thanks to friend, Coach John Calipari, and neighbor, Andy Melder, who were the first to read my writing when it was in the early stages and offer suggestions.

Thanks to long-time friend and prolific author, Pat Williams, for encouraging me to try to publish the book and to suggest Advantage Media Group, who had published six of his works. Founder Adam Witty runs a great ship and I am indebted to the early encouragement of editor, Denis Boyles, who believed I had a book, even when I had my doubts. Thanks to the help of editors Brooke White and Mike Walker, and the total team action of Kim Hall, Alison Morse and the art production of George Stevens. All were very good encouragers.

Of course, I am indebted to my wife Ann and family for the support and love they have given me for these many years; we are talking about five children—Larry, Alex, Stan, Carey Ann and Dominic—and nine grandkids. Thanks also to the many relationships formed with those who played on teams I coached and who coached with me. I am so honored to be able to say that many of those players and coaches have become true vintage friends—some for fifty years, some for forty, others for thirty, twenty and more recent times. Special bonds are made when teams work together that set them apart.

As I have passed through life, there have been so many that have contributed to my spiritual development directly and indirectly. Upon the death of my parents five weeks apart in 1998, I was moved to re-dedicate my life with the hope of finishing strong. Regrettably, I had wandered away from my faith base to varying degrees; but hearing people tell me of all the contributions they made to others in the small town of Plainfield, IN, where they spent most of their lives, inspired me greatly.

At that point, Dr. Steve Faubion of the Calvary Christian Church in Pacific Palisades, CA became my pastor, mentor and friend. Our son Dominic was already attending the Calvary elementary school. Steve helped guide me and my wife, Ann, toward a new level. He set up a great small group of which he and his wife, Suzie, also became a part. Listening to radio pastors on Christian radio that included teachers such as Charles Swindoll, Tony Evans, Greg Laurie, Chuck Smith, Raul Reis, Bill Ritchie and others were of great encouragement. Then there were the writings of men like Max Lucado, Josh McDowell, Philip Yancey, and Swindoll. I was privileged to get to talk with Max and Josh as well. In addition there was a great Bible study led by a wonderful teacher and friend, the late Allen Landry, associate pastor at Crenshaw Christian Center that had such a great influence on my re-direction. The world suffered a great loss when cancer claimed Allen so early in his life.

I was fortunate that my next move was to Dallas, a veritable spiritual center, where I came under the influence of the brilliant teacher, RReach mission founder, Dr. Ramesh Richard, as well as the brilliant preacher/writer Tony Evans, my eloquent pastor Pete Briscoe, pastor Jack Graham and others.

Here I would love to thank my several vintage friends (that I call anyone who has known me ten years or more and still likes me), but I would leave someone out and we would both feel bad. There is little that is so special as long-time friends, and if you are one of these and your name starts with one of the letters in the alphabet, I am talking about you. Finally thanks to Milligan College for the base they helped me establish, to Earlham College who gave me a chance to be a college coach, to Hope International University for their encouragement, and to Dallas Christian for the opportunity to teach again.

PREFACE

THE FOUR-STEP SYSTEM FOR BEING A BETTER INFLUENCE ON LIFE-TEAMS

At the outset, please understand that this is not a book about basketball, though there are a number of basketball and sports stories I use as metaphors that will interest the sports fan. It does concern coaching, but only in the sense that I believe we are all called to be coaches to others as we go through life. However, I think a sports-oriented person will enjoy this book, because we will draw from many sports analogies with which I am most familiar, having coached in the NBA for many years.

Here are some terms I think are important:

ON POINT: We need to be "on point" as mentors or encouragers to others in times of need.

LIFE-TEAMS: The groups in which we play a role, helping attain a shared goal, are the teams we form in daily life. These are everywhere in our lives in different contexts: family, corporate, institutional, and community.

INFLUENCE QUOTIENT: The Influence Quotient in this book refers to a specific kind of intelligence: the ability to influence our teams for a positive outcome. The higher the Influence Quotient, the better.

FOUR-STEP SYSTEM: The purpose of this book is to present, from a Christian perspective, the Four-Step System for building better relationships within the various Life-Teams in which we are all members.

We naturally prefer that the various teams we join provide good experiences. No one aspires to be on a losing team. The Four-Step System, described as a metaphor based on four wheels, is intended for all who desire to improve their Influence Quotient with their various Life-Teams. This approach is different from the usual leadership mandates set out in so many books. We cannot all be leaders all the time, which would negate the concept of a team. But we do need to be good influences on others. Developing our Influence Quotient will enable us to be more effective within our teams and help us develop better team relationships as a result. When you embark on this process, you should reap the bonus benefit of improving your leadership skills as well.

FOREWORD

BY AVIS STEWART

FORMER PLAYER, VP EARLHAM COLLEGE, IN

I n September of 2011, Del Harris was awarded the Distinguished Service Award by Earlham College—a small prestigious liberal arts college in Richmond, IN. The recipient of this coveted award must reflect honor through his/her life achievements and demonstrate excellence throughout one's career. It is not awarded on an annual basis, and is given at the discretion of the college to a committed servant leader. The evening before Del received this honor, many of his former players came together to reminisce about our time under his guidance as a college coach from 1965 to 1974--before he became the well-known, highly acclaimed NBA Coach of the Houston Rockets, Milwaukee Bucks and Los Angeles Lakers, Coach of the 2004 Chinese National Team, and international coach.

This Earlham gathering of Del's former players was fun, filled with love and laughter, and provided an opportunity for us to share our life stories with each other. As each vignette was shared, it became apparent that the life principles that Del had instilled in us as 18 to 22 year old college students are the same ones that he has lived and taught as a NBA Coach, international basketball icon, or loving and caring husband and father. Each story was different; but similar, as they all evolved around the concepts of building meaningful life relationships.

The Distinguished Service Award that Del received the following day was for the many noteworthy accomplishments he has made to the game of basketball. However, what was more evident was how he has used his success as a basketball icon to share a kind, thoughtful message about building lasting, life-changing relationships.

Earlier that year, on a national stage, Athletes in Action honored Del at the NBA All-Star Game as a servant leader by awarding him the Jerry Colangelo Award—a coveted honor given to a person of outstanding integrity, character, and leadership. This award and the Earlham College Distinguished Service Award recognize Del's *Influence Quotient—the ability to be of influence for good on one's family/ team/organization, regardless of the role*—and his passion and commitment to the team-building message that he has shared throughout his career.

These two servant leadership, life-achievement based awards illustrate the message Del Harris communicates through *On Point*. The essence of this approach is the construction of lifelong, rewarding relationships that are established through a formal method. This scripturally-based, proven process provided my Earlham College teammates and me, as well as nationally and internationally renowned athletes, coaches, and executives with a foundation that allowed us to improve our *Influence Quotient* as good teammates, colleagues, community leaders, parents, and role players in life.

As a lifelong friend and a member of one of Del Harris' championship teams, my life, my family's lives, and those lives in the community in which I reside have been enriched by the concepts Del shares through *On Point*—one of the most compelling, well-structured approaches to our roles as *influencers* in today's society. Those seeking to improve their *Influence Quotient,* and live a more resolute, purposeful life will benefit immensely from carefully reading and actively applying this agape-filled method described in *On Point.* This systematic process from mission to unity and meaningful relationships will prove to be an epiphany to many, and will bring joy and thanksgiving to those willing to adhere to it. I encourage and invite you to read it; actively live it; and then reap the benefits of what it means to be a humble, yet influential, individual who serves *on point* of a unified, highly successful family/team/organization.

TABLE OF CONTENTS

INTRODUCTION

BEING ON POINT: DEVELOPING THE POINT-GUARD CONCEPT WITHIN YOU

Let me explain briefly how this book came into being and why the metaphor of the point guard makes sense to me.

I have been coaching basketball at every level for more than a half-century. For more than thirty years, I have coached NBA teams such as the Dallas Mavericks, Houston Rockets, Milwaukee Bucks, Los Angeles Lakers, and Chicago Bulls, and, like other sports personalities, from time to time I'm invited to speak at various events.

One event in particular inspired this book. I was asked to be the principal speaker at the presentation of the Nancy Lieberman Award in Detroit in the spring of 2010. This annual award honors the student-athlete selected as the best point guard of the season in NCAA Division I Women's Basketball. Knowing that I would be speaking to a lot more people than just the recipient, Andrea Riley of the University of Oklahoma, I pondered ideas that would be meaningful to Andrea but might have some value for the rest of the audience as well. It occurred to me that the point guard is central to building a great basketball team. So I began to examine the elements this position requires if a team is to play its best game. Since we are all on "teams" of various kinds, the translation flowed naturally from the traits a successful basketball point guard must have to the traits we all need to become "on point" in various Life-Team situations.

I began to list the qualities I looked for in my point guards as well as what I saw in other successful point guards. To be effective at this position demands more from a player than simply executing fundamental basketball skills. The good point guards exhibit important personality traits that are as important to the success of his or her team as physical basketball skills. It became obvious to me that anyone seeking to be successful in a competitive environment would benefit greatly from harvesting many of these same accessible qualities. The question, then, became, how do we cultivate these attributes? The Four-Step System, presented as four wheels containing six spokes each, provides a good answer to that question.

Whether we are the *de facto* team leader or a role player, each of us would like our Life-Teams to be winning ones, and we should want to influence that end instead of being passive observers. Our goal should be to improve our Influence Quotient as opposed to pushing to be the leader in every situation. The emphasis should be on acknowledging the value of every teammate's role while helping them prepare for times when they will need to step to the front to influence an outcome. Incorporating the elements of the Four-Step System provides the momentum necessary to move toward successful team experiences. It can be implemented to help an individual not only influence others, but also improve personally as he increases his Influence Quotient. The end game is to improve the performance of our Life-Teams by cultivating meaningful relationships.

Del Harris
Dallas 2012

WHAT'S SO SPECIAL ABOUT THE POINT GUARD'S ROLE IN BASKETBALL AND HOW CAN I USE IT?

T o begin, we will examine several important aspects that a quality basketball point guard must possess, and then in the following chapters we will see how those character- istics are ones we can develop to become capable "point persons" on our Life-Teams. I believe there is a point guard within each of us who can provide opportunities to make our Life-Teams more successful. We will examine ways to make our teams better, using the basketball idiom I am most familiar with as a base from which to draw analogies. In the process we will refer to being "on point" in any arena of life as synonymous to being a point guard on the basketball court.

We are destined to be members of multiple Life-Teams that will change as we traverse life: our families, our schools, our churches, service organizations, neighborhood groups, and so forth. A homo- geneous grouping of any kind needs those who utilize skills similar to those of a basketball point guard. We will study the Four-Step System, which is based on personality traits that can help unify an organization and ultimately develop successful relationships among team members.

Develop the point guard within you: The point guard in basketball is the one who is largely in control of the basketball, particularly in the most defining moments of a game. It becomes his or her responsibility to get the ball to the right player, or in some instances, to become that particular player, the one who takes the defining shot. These situations develop when individuals encounter decisive moments in their personal or professional lives and realize they must be "on point." While this book is not focused primarily on leadership, you can use the principles it advocates when you cannot rely on the leadership of others. With that in mind, we will take the role of a basketball point guard as a launching pad to offer practical and spiritual principles that anyone can apply to successful team building. We will use the term Influence Quotient to denote the quality that equates roughly with leadership skills in someone who isn't necessarily a designated or recognized leader. That person may develop into a leader in time, but his or her goal is to be a good influence on others, not to become crowned as the king of the hill in every situation. That particular approach would be counterproductive to the team concept, in my opinion. Just look at what happens in our political system when people fight one another to become leaders.

A point guard commits to a mission: In the case of the basketball team, the coach and players must determine short- and long-term goals that the team seeks to accomplish. As the one who controls the offense and is the lead attacker on the defense, a point guard has to commit totally to his team's mission. They must do their best to get the rest of the team to do so as well. They set the tone for everyone by their actions and attitude. This is the starting point that will allow all the other things required of the position to fall in place. Without this commitment, the entire process is likely to fall short. Of course, to be successful in any endeavor, you must define a mission for which you feel a measure of passion, a mission you can commit to accomplishing.

Our Point Guard President: In 2009, at the beginning of President Obama's mission as the leader of the United States, I was an assistant coach for the Chicago Bulls. Prior to his election, the President had spent his years in Chicago. He is an avid sports fan, especially of basketball. So, in February, shortly after he took office, he allowed our team a special meet-and-greet with him. Such meetings are usually reserved for the NBA champion at the end of a season, or at the start of the next, but we were his home team and in town to play the Washington Wizards, so we got an early invite. I planned what to say if I got an opening to speak directly to him.

I had purchased one of his autobiographical books and, after waiting in line with team players to get an autograph, I handed him the book and jumped in quickly with my well-rehearsed advice that went pretty much as follows: "Mr. President, I have coached basketball for fifty years, and I know of your love for the game. You are the only person elected by the majority of the people in our country and, as such, you are our point guard. I would like to give you my coaching advice about that position." (I have his attention now and he has a big smile on his face, so I know I am good to go and security is not on the way.)

"As a point guard," I continued, "you have to know your teammates' strengths and weaknesses, and my suggestion is that you not pass the ball to [House Speaker, Nancy] Pelosi or [Senate Majority Leader, Harry] Reid unless you are sure they are in the right position."

The president had a good laugh and replied, "You might have a good point there."

Unfortunately, he did pass the ball to them shortly thereafter when he had them formulate and initiate a health-care revision bill. They fumbled, and then air-balled so badly that the president had to take the ball back and try to accomplish it with a different approach. It turned out to be a tough game for him either way, but I had tried my best to help. And no, he hasn't called.

The best point guards are serving-leaders

That is, they lead by serving their teammates first of all. This entails developing a deep humility quotient without sacrificing confidence. None of the rest of the qualities needed in a point guard, or person on point, will work if that person does not understand the power of humility. A combination of true humility with a healthy self-esteem that is aware of the needs of others is vital. Without it, you will not be able to serve consistently or continue to influence others. With a spirit of humility you can draw others to you and begin to lead, at times without being aware of it.

In the game of basketball all eyes are on the point guard. His or her teammates look to him or her to get them the ball. It all begins with the point guard. If point guards are unwilling to give, teams cannot function. Therefore, good point guards start from an "others-oriented position." They have to know their teammates, their abilities, their preferences, and even their mentalities to serve them well. On basketball teams, as well as in the real world, people on point need to get to know those around them and learn what their concerns are. When point guards know what their teammates need, they can serve them, build them up, and help them be better at their roles. As we analyze the skills and responsibilities of the point guard, it will become obvious that we all have the capability to draw from within ourselves these same attributes in order to become effective point persons in our own lives. Willingness to serve with humility is key, along with the confidence that comes through commitment to a worthy mission.

Point guards demonstrate they care about their teammates

Point guards' willingness and ability to get to know their teammates are of utmost importance to the point guards' success. This comes about naturally when they forgo basic self-centeredness and seek to find ways to show concern for their teammates. It would be difficult to overemphasize this requisite for becoming a successful person on point in any arena of life. Not everyone is equally likeable, so it may be necessary to make a conscious effort to act out concern for "difficult" people until genuine concern becomes a reality. This is a big part of serving. Point guards have to demonstrate concern for teammates before teammates open up and reveal the personal struggles or internal angst that may be affecting their performance. Concern must be established.

The point guard represents a higher power

You will readily see where this will go when I refer to spiritual applications. Staying with sports for the moment, however, point guards represent the power of the coach. They call the plays that the coach has taught or may have called for in a particular situation. In the dynamics of team basketball, point guards perform as the conduit between coaches and other team members. They are often referred to as "the coach on the court." As the coach, I always tried to communicate well with my point guards, and hoped to have a close relationship with them. I would trust them to call a lot of the plays after we had discussed what plays to emphasize for that game or for a particular situation after a time-out. Everything functioned best when we were in agreement regarding such issues as to whom we should try to get the ball for various reasons—maybe to a player with a weaker defender, or to one whose defender was in trouble with a foul. My point guard would understand whom we should keep happy and productive by making sure that player got enough touches and shots. When we were sputtering, or when I decided I should take responsibility, I would step in and call plays. But regardless of my call, the point man would try to see that it happened. He would try to do my will. This is exactly what the believer is trying to do in his relationship with the highest of powers, the triune God. This is why Paul referred to believers as ambassadors, representatives of a higher power (2 Cor. 5:20).

Point guards communicate; they spread the word

They do this in various ways when they do their jobs well. They have verbal calls and hand signals that communicate the plan to teammates on any given play action. Everything tends to sputter or fall apart if the point guard does not commit to communicating with the coach and passing the coach's message on to the team. The point guard's unselfish and encouraging attitude can influence the attitude of the entire group. That is a good start, but the point guard is at his effective best when persistent, reminding teammates of their mission and getting their commitment to the program. The point guard is an encourager and a team builder. Certainly the spiritual allegory is quite apparent here.

Consider Magic Johnson of the champion Lakers of the 1980s era as a great example of someone who did these things as a true point guard, leading the Lakers to five NBA championships. He was a positive and encouraging influencer who kept his team focused on their immediate and long-term goals. He made his coach, Pat Riley, famous in the process—that and the hair.

Being on the point brings responsibility

Good point guards must not only fulfill their performance role but also use the rapport they establish with teammates to get to know them better in order to address their concerns before destructive issues develop into team cancers. Players will sometimes seek to divorce themselves from the team when things go badly and promote themselves as the answer to the team's problems. A point man must be effective in keeping team chemistry in balance. He will encourage the individual who is feeling discouraged and continue to strive to maintain team unity. This same dynamic occurs daily in businesses, homes, churches, and other institutions. It takes someone who is prepared and ready to be influential to step to the front and prevent a potentially devastating confrontation. We must all prepare to be that peacemaker on our Life-Teams.

It can be a daunting task to hold a team together through the ups and downs of a long season. The most successful NBA teams lose in the neighborhood of twenty to thirty games a season. That is nearly an entire season's worth of games for a college or high-school team. It is roughly a month of days that bring disappointment to all the fans and nationwide critical analysis in print as well as from the squawking heads on television and sports talk radio. Seldom does anyone get spared when even the best teams lose three or four games in a short period of time. This is why more than one person must be prepared to be on point at any time, and why it is important to develop team-building concepts within one's team or organization. This same dynamic transpires when corporations, churches, and families go through rough patches. The more people who prepare themselves to be influential in the tough times, the better the chances for the team to stay intact.

A point guard's personal goals must complement the team's goals

It is not selfish for each player to have personal goals. However, each individual's purpose should align with the overall team mission. This is especially true of the person on point, though each player must practice and play in ways that are consistent with the overall objective.

All the top performers dreamed of individual successes before they achieved them. This is not a selfish act. Each individual must harbor personal ambitions. These images stir a player to make the extra effort in practices as well as make various sacrifices in outside activities and choices. The winning players constantly push themselves to improve. They set short-range targets for themselves as measuring sticks. If one area of their game has slipped over the past few games, they set goals to improve in the upcoming games. While common purpose is the essence of a mission, each role-player needs individual aims to help drive him or her and the mission forward. Improved individual performances energize the team and give support to the mission.

However, point guards can never let desire for selfish personal statistics override responsibility to the team. They have the ball and are in a perfect position to take every shot, but they cannot do that. They have to maintain their integrity for their team to be at its best. Their goals must coincide with what is best for their team, and they cannot let false rationalizations and temptations of personal glory interfere with that. Every organization must have someone who will step forward to help keep the mission going. That is what is done by anyone who wants to be a good influence on a Life-Team.

A point guard is introspective, but must be honest

Good point guards must be realistic about their abilities in order to improve. They look at results in an objective way. They study game film of themselves to evaluate their strengths and weaknesses. They evaluate their decision making, knowing that this defines their overall grasp of their role. Learning about ourselves is an important step in the process of gathering information as we prepare for the tasks in our mission. It is an operation that generally proves to be quite difficult. Many studies have demonstrated the absurdity of people's attempts at self-evaluation. Almost any group of subjects involved in self-analysis studies rates itself staggeringly well above average. Usually, an inordinate percentage of group members will place themselves in the top 10 percent in most categories being ranked. Obviously, 50 percent of people cannot realistically rank in the top 10 percent of any endeavor, but that is about the number of people who think they do. This is true of students, teachers, pastors, and businessmen.

Humility tends to have a low rank on the human to-do list. We really don't lack self-esteem as much as we are led to believe.

Okay, so you want some real metrics. In his book, *When the Game is Over, It All Goes Back in the Box*, Daniel Ortberg highlights studies that speak directly to our predilection for self-deception.[1] In one survey, 800,000 high-school students were asked to rate themselves above or below average in social skills. Obviously, a true breakdown would end up with a roughly 50–50 divide. However, all 800,000 rated themselves above average and 25 percent said they were in the top 1 percent. In another survey 88 percent of college professors rated themselves above average. Out of 200 sociologists, more than 100 rated themselves in the top 10 percent in the world. In another survey 90 percent of pastors rated themselves in the top half as well. The picture is pretty clear.

In this context it is easy to see that point guards who are not realistic and honest in their self-evaluation may find fault with everyone else when things are not going well. They can blame the big players for not rebounding, the shooters for missing shots, the other players for not defending, or the coach for being inept. Obviously, this kind of thinking will defeat them and their teams. Certainly, good point guards will not be blind to the errors of others and will try to motivate them to do better, but they will examine themselves and see, first of all, what they can do to help matters. This is what each Life-Team needs from its members, and the more team members who can develop this quality in themselves, the more likely the team will improve. One person can make a difference, and several people with a common aim can perform miracles.

---

1   Ortberg, John. *When the Game Is Over*. Grand Rapids, MI: Zondervan, 2007, 119–120.

The point guard will enlist the help of others

Beyond honest self-criticism, point guards who are serious about becoming the best will work with the coaching staff and/or respected teammates in evaluating their performance. Often, they will have a shooting partner or workout buddy who amounts to an account-ability partner, to help keep them in line with their shot, work ethic, and overall purpose. A good example of this partnership is the one between Steve Nash and Dirk Nowitzki, who helped each other win three NBA MVP awards between them. Steve worked tirelessly alongside Dirk, while playing with the Dallas Mavericks, before he left for Phoenix. Jason Terry replaced Steve as Dirk's partner at that time. But the work Steve and Dirk did together paid off later with MVP awards for both men. The work of Dirk and Jason led to an NBA championship for them as well. They were the best 1–2, fourth-quarter punch in the league in their championship season of 2011. Two are better than one. "When one falls, the other can pull him up" is the concept (Eccl. 4:9–10). This is evidence of the point guard's humility quotient and how he or she must always understand that even the best of leaders needs help.

The point guard must evaluate the competition

As if all these responsibilities to their teams were not enough, point guards also have to study the tendencies of their opponents. They must know the basics of their opponents' offense and defensive style. They have to study the strengths and weaknesses of their opponents' individual match-up, which they will have to defend, as well as those of other players they may defend during the game. They need to know who should be fouled late in the game because of that player's inability to make free throws. They must identify the weaker links in a player's defense and know how to exploit them. Like all of us in various areas of life, the point man needs to be knowledgeable about the competition, that is, the "enemy." Many of the enemies of the basketball team will not be seven-foot centers or lightning-fast scorers, but spiritual in nature: selfishness, jealousy, deceit, and lies. We meet a variety of competitors and opponents in life, but the ones that demand the most attention in our families, businesses, and churches are spiritual in nature. Point people must be aware and alert.

Work to be an effective point person, even as a role player

As noted earlier, not every person can be the leader of the team. The very definition of "team" prevents that. And not every point person will be the one designated as the point guard, like Magic Johnson. To show that anyone can take the bull by the horns and assume the role of the point when needed, consider a player who went far beyond that—Michael Jordan. He became the best-known Chicago Bull of them all. At the game's moment of truth, Michael would take the ball in his hands and orchestrate the finish of close games, and he won six championships with that ability. Recently, players such as Kobe Bryant, Dwayne Wade, LeBron James, Tim Duncan, and Dirk Nowitzki, who are not full-time point guards, have stepped up at the moment of truth to win championships. To have a great team, someone must fill the point-person leadership role and get the rest of the team on board at key times. The tragedy at the World Trade Towers in 2001 produced a great number of people who did wonderful point-person acts but who started the day as everyday role players to illustrate that point.

Super Bowl XLV

A great example of how a player can step into a leadership role at the moment of truth occurred at Super Bowl XLV in 2011. The acknowledged leader of the team was the veteran Charles Woodson, but he broke his collarbone in the first half and had to miss the rest of the game. Although Charles gave an impassioned speech at half-time that helped inspire the team, it was up to quarterback Aaron Rodgers— normally a quiet person—to assert himself as *de facto* leader in the second half. Aaron did that in grand style and was named MVP of the game because he set the point person within him free when they needed him.

Ironically, the same opportunity presented itself on the other side of the ball for the Packers as well. The leading defensive players for Green Bay—Donald Driver and Charles Woodson—both got injured, with the Packers holding a slim 21–17 lead at half-time. In the third quarter, the Packers' defensive coordinator approached the young defensive back, Clay Matthews, and told him that he would have to be the man to take charge on the field. Clay led a key defensive stand in the third quarter by batting down a pass by Steelers' quarterback Ben Roethlisberger, and in the fourth quarter, Clay made a hard tackle that shook the ball loose for a fumble. That play set up the deciding touchdown that gave the Pack a 28–17 lead that would stand up for the victory. Having grown up in a family of professional football players, Matthews was prepared and ready to take over as the point person in time of need. As a result, he was named the Defensive Player of the Game.

Learning must be continuous

While accumulating knowledge is an essential element in preparation, your humility must remain intact. As someone once said, "It is what I learned after I thought I knew everything that made me successful." Human beings generally face the danger of becoming too attached to what we have come to consider the "right way" to act or to think in certain circumstances. Though it is important to hold on dearly to proven moral and ethical truths, we need to maintain an openness and willingness to learn as well. An athlete, coach, businessperson, or parent who loses the desire to search for deeper or broader understanding will cease to grow. Once the passion to expand our borders dies, we begin to wither. As we move forward in life, our goal should always be to continue to learn and be flexible in our attitudes and behavior, without violating our moral compass.

The approach here will be to connect chains of actions and attitudes in the form of wheels that can enable an individual to increase his or her Influence Quotient and become an effective point person. The four wheels, each containing six elements or "spokes," will move us along the path from mission commitment to the forming and maintaining of satisfying relationships.

STUDY

1. On a scale of 1–10, how do you rate yourself in your ability to select a goal and follow through on it for a month? A year? In the process, think of something that you achieved for which you had planned. You may be better than you think.

2. Write down a faith mission for your life in one page or less. This will help when you read the next chapter.

3. Read 2 Cor. 5:20. How does this relate to being God's "point guard on the court"?

4. This week try to acquaint yourself better with someone in one of your immediate Life-Teams so that you can understand that person better. Seek to focus your conversation on that person instead of yourself and see how much easier that approach makes toward understanding the other person.

5. How prepared are you to give a ready answer, as noted in 1 Peter 3:15, "Always be prepared to give an answer to everyone who asks you to give the reason for the hope that you have. But do this with gentleness and respect." You always need to be ready to defend your mission and spread the word of the higher power we are expected to represent—the coach, the company or God the Father.

CHAPTER TWO

LEARNING TO BE ON POINT INSIDE AND OUT

Being influential comes ahead of seeking leadership

The problem is that some people try to force their way to the front and they push people away from them instead. Leading is not only something to be learned but earned. We have already addressed the first step, and that is to show concern for others while being willing to be a servant, as a point guard in basketball must do. To be a person on point naturally implies the development of some level of leadership skills nonetheless. Effective leadership starts from the inside and works outward. It begins by making certain internal commitments.

Almost every author I have read or listened to, relative to the study of leadership, makes this point. While we will discuss leadership from various angles, let us say that "keeping it simple" is always a good foundation for such discourses. When my lifelong friend died, former Indiana state senator Tom Hession, I reflected on his exemplary life in such a light. One of my main comments was, "Leaders of influence have a strong, integrated character and care deeply for others, which is demonstrated through active servant leadership. Tom lived that his entire life." He typified this statement in his life, and I believe this is a good definition of leadership and being on point. Leading came easily and apparently naturally to Tom. Caring was his calling card.

I can suggest alternative definitions of leadership. The two main definitions I would select are the following:

1. The quality in a person that enables him or her to guide and influence others in terms of their behavior and opinions.

2. A quality so complex that it has more characteristics than there are locks in a federal prison; dozens of experts have supplied as many as seventy characteristics, all said to be absolute keys to opening the "locks" of this quality.

If you detect a bit of sarcasm in the second definition, it is not out of disrespect for the topic or for those who have tried to corral it. It simply points to the depth and breadth to which the inquisitive have gone to find the best way to present this important life issue.

Having noted the high regard for the enormity of the subject of leadership, we are not totally overwhelmed by it. Our approach here will be to combine multiple characteristics in four related wheels in an effort to simplify the subject to some extent and still capture much of its depth. It is my hope that by presenting some thoughts from an athletic perspective, along with strong scriptural support, we may shed a bit of new light on the subject. We reluctantly go forward where many have trod. We will combine personal thoughts with ideas from experts in the field, and assign elements from the athletic, secular, and spiritual domains as they apply to team building and relationships. Hopefully, this will prove helpful to those seeking to improve themselves in these important areas of life because leadership is a learnable skill and a major factor in influencing our Life-Teams.

Internal transactions are reflected in the first wheel of the system: The diagram that follows illustrates the first of the four wheels that we will present in our study. The initial *passion* for a mission must be followed by intelligent *preparation*, the gathering of knowledge through study and experience. Knowledge promotes the *confidence* to move ahead. *Enthusiasm* breeds the *patience* to endure setbacks and difficulties. Following this process with *persistence* enables us to find *creative* ways to execute whatever it takes to complete our intended goal or mission. The wheel below should be followed clockwise.

These qualities are what a good basketball point guard will master and they are the same qualities that most experts say are required for point leaders in any arena of life. These are not isolated entities that can be developed separately. They cannot stand alone or even be followed out of order and still be effective, in my opinion. They are interrelated, connective parts that work together to produce a great result within someone who is striving to reach a goal or achieve a mission.

For example, one cannot start in the middle of the circle by focusing on patience and expect to reach a great goal. Someone who isn't prepared will certainly need patience, because he will probably not achieve much at all without laying a foundation of information. He may wait a lifetime. Patience won't develop in a vacuum, nor will persistence. There is a domino effect in this process, as one characteristic in the wheel follows another, feeding off the former spoke and supplying energy to the next. While an argument can be made that one of the above elements is more vital than another, you cannot isolate any element from the foundational elements that precede it or the other elements that flow after it. This wheel represents the internal starter in the series of the four wheels that must be developed for someone to become the most effective championship point person on any of his Life-Teams.

Evaluating your Influence Quotient

What am I doing to become more capable of leading, which means being able to influence others? How can I know if I am influencing others? The true test of leadership at any level is whether you are able to command a following for any significant length of time, relative to actions or ideas you espouse. Ask yourself if people want to know what your plans are before they decide on a course of action. Do people tend to come to your way of thinking in a conversation without your hammering them into the ground? Are there people in your school, workplace, church, home, or other group who seek your opinion often? Occasionally? If the answer to these questions is positive, you are already having some effect as a leader. You are an influencer depending on how often you answer yes. If the answer is a no, or "not often," you can draw a clear conclusion.

Maybe your team members agree with you, or follow you, for a while, but they don't stay with you. This is common. Obviously, the need for integrity comes to the front early in any such discussion, because a good leader must be consistent. Having integrity means to be at one on the inside and the outside. What a person does must be congruent with what he espouses. He has to "walk his talk," and that springs from within. A short circuit usually occurs when your actions betray your words, or it may result if others come to believe that you don't really care enough about them and their opinions.

To be on point, know the person you want to be

At the outset we noted the value in formulating a worthy mission statement, and in the study suggestions at the end of Chapter One, I recommended that you draw up a one-page mission plan. Many of you have done that previously in your life because this is certainly not a new concept. But if you are like most people, you do not revisit your mission statement often. As we advance and grow, there will be many changes in our personal landscapes, so we need to keep our mission statement current and meaningful. Knowing who and what you want to be requires prayerful consideration on the believer's part.

We live in a world of rapid change—our cell phones and computers, which become outdated seemingly overnight, are not the only examples. Our human psyches do not go unscathed in this era of accelerated transition. To avoid lengthy personal "dry spells" of various types we must maintain our passion for our goals and current activities. Without the continuing passion and commitment to a purpose, our employment becomes just a job, a boring task to be fulfilled out of duty or economic necessity. The same excitement can fade from our outside activities as well. Our spirits tend to perish when we lack passion for a vision. We usually end up doing what has to be done, but we lack the joy and creativity that come with doing what excites us. Still, passion for the best of missions needs balance. *Do not confuse obsessive, addictive behavior for passion.*

It helps to get involved in work and activities you like to do

It is nearly impossible to be a person on point if you are in an environment in which you feel uncomfortable. I was fortunate to be able to work for more than fifty years in a kid's game—basketball. To put it in perspective, there are 435 US representatives in Congress and only thirty NBA head coaches, and each has an equally tenuous job-retention situation. These jobs are hard to attain and difficult to keep. It was amazing over the years how many successful businessmen who owned great homes and had good families would get excited talking to me about my "job." Quite often these were people who had achieved the ultimate in their fields. I got the message many times, either overtly or subtly, that they would trade positions with me in a minute, had that been possible. They liked what their work had provided for them, but they would have preferred to go to the gym every day and to the arena that night to run the sidelines than sit through another board meeting. Many tended to retire when they had the opportunity, and the happier ones would find something they really liked to do after that. That new activity may have paid a lot less money, or even nothing, but it came as a result of a passion and gained them more personal fulfillment than being a CEO.

Finding work that coincides with one's personal interests gives you the best chance for job contentment. Short of that, performing an outside function, preferably service-oriented, that stirs passion, may be the best answer. One's creativity opens up more in these situations, and in the process it gives one the satisfying ability to be influential. Bob Buford's books entitled, *Game Plan* and *Half Time*, contain wonderful analyses of people who did exactly these things in their lives after successful professional careers.

A good point person will demonstrate enthusiasm

Enthusiastic people draw others to them. People like to be around this type of person as opposed to doom-and-gloom naysayers. We invariably pay high regard to those who demonstrate a sustained excitement for what they do, so long as they are not just boastful and clanging cymbals, of course. This quality alone tends to set a person up to be a potential leader. Anyone can be enthusiastic for thirty seconds or minutes or days, even manic-depressives manage that, but a true leader must have a deep passion for the mission to sustain a *joie de vivre* in his work and to affect others significantly. That is, some of the most loathed people in history, as well as the best of us—from Hitler to Mother Teresa, from Stalin to Gandhi—asserted massive influence due to an enthusiastic commitment to their purpose. For good or for evil, such is the power of enthusiasm.

Enthusiasm pays

Dick Vitale was a pretty good college coach at the University of Detroit back in the 1970s, good enough to become head coach of the Detroit Pistons for a time. He was not as successful in the NBA, but basketball and people remained his passions. He soon found employment behind the ESPN microphone when they opened the studio in 1979. He has remained there for decades. He had a face for radio—sorry, Dick—and became a multimillionaire star on television with his enthusiastic basketball broadcasts, and he became an in-demand speaker on college campuses. Dick's bombastic approach to his work as broadcaster and his passion for the sport of basketball and life itself reverberates on TV screens. He has lifted the spirits of millions of people for almost five decades.

How did he do this? Vitale was prepared, knowledgeable, and had a passion for the game while exhibiting a love of people. He became a megastar with what flowed from him perpetually—"Enthusiasm, baby!" He is persistent, and it is his passion and enthusiasm that allow him to have such stick-to-it-iveness. An obvious aura of joy surrounds him that makes you wonder if he ever has a down day. Of course he does, but his mental approach seems not to allow it to linger. He leads with enthusiasm. Many sportscasters have since followed his lead, copying his style to varying degrees.

Luke 10:27 advises us to love the Lord our God with all our heart, with all our soul, with all our strength and with all our mind. God wants more than just an intellectual response (mind) and more than actions (strength). The "heart" and "soul" speak to the emotional part—the passion and enthusiasm. God wants the entire chain reaction within us. The point person must give it all to get others to commit to the team mission as well.

Mission choice alone is not enough

To quickly review the first wheel, we note that having chosen a mission we can be truly passionate about at the outset, we must commit to following it up with solid preparation, mentally and physically. While gathering information is vital in terms of supporting the chosen goal, it is not sufficient to sustain anyone through the inevitable ups and downs of most endeavors. However, as preparation and information gathering increase, the path to the end vision becomes clearer. This renews enthusiasm and creates an environment for the patience required to pursue the goal. Without patience, which is key to endurance, it is impossible to acquire the persistence to overcome the hurdles that will inevitably arise. At this point, *sometimes just before conceding defeat,* the one who forges ahead will come up with a creative solution that will enable him to execute his mission. These are the first of a series of steps that must be taken. Without them, the mission is not a goal. It is only a wish or dream that has little likelihood of reaching fulfillment. But there is more.

There must be integrity between purpose and action

The first wheel focuses on things that you must do *internally* to become a person on point, one who affects his team in a positive manner and who increases his Influence Quotient. The second, third, and fourth wheels center on characteristics that must be demonstrated to others—*external* actions, evidence of what is internal.

Remember the description of the point guard and how he had to be willing to be a servant and show concern for others? That all begins on the inside with the concepts in the first wheel. The action in the second wheel starts when that commitment to being others-oriented is demonstrated. Proving that you care is the first piece of evidence that must be exhibited on the outside.

It sounds simple, but it is very difficult for most people to do this. The reason is that we all begin our lives with an attitude of *I want what I want when I want it*, and we find it hard to break away from that pattern. Certainly, we all recall enough of our childhood to remember that our parents had to *teach us to share*. It did not happen naturally. Those of you who are parents and hopefully infinitely proud of your adult children will nonetheless recall the stress of administering these lessons in your children's formative years. Self-centeredness is a function of what Paul described as "our sinful nature." (Rom. 7:18) To overcome this requires sustained effort and is a lifelong process for us as human beings.

Adding on the second wheel— Authentic caring:

This is our front-wheel drive, moving everything forward. It sets up the chain reactions shown on the diagram of the second wheel. As individuals perform their roles on a team, in a family, or in a business, they must establish *operational relationships*. These relationships may grow as people acknowledge their *interdependence* with other team members. People on all sides will acknowledge the value of others to at least a functional extent. People who express a degree of *humility* and are willing to acknowledge such dependence will generate reasonably effective *communication* with the team.

As we work our way around the wheel, we see that each point feeds on the one prior to it. In a caring environment, it is easy for an individual to do his or her part to keep it all moving forward. As each person continues to show appreciation for the value of others' contributions, communication becomes easier and more frequent. This engenders the potential for *continuing cooperation.* The team members become more comfortable and work together to promote a successful outcome in this scenario. People see that the system works and this provides *validation* for what they are doing individually and as a unit. And this is just at the halfway mark in our Four-Step System, but it is easy to see how progress can be made. Let us examine the second wheel a little more closely.

Interpreting the second wheel

Too many times I have said to myself, "I should have called" or "I wish I had thought of that" when I saw another perform some type of service or another. I have known people who seemed to start out the day with their antennas up, looking for ways to serve. They are like what we call a "pass-first" point guard in basketball. They make a lot more assists than the average point guard. Far too often, I would describe myself as a "shoot first" point guard, looking out for my own interests. The admonition in both the Old Testament and New Testament to be *others-directed* is quite clear. Jesus called loving God and one another as the fulfillment of the law and the prophets (Matt. 7:12 and 22:40). He described these as the most important of the commands (Matt. 19:19). Simply stated, that means if you love, you will not break moral law by stealing, lying, or committing criminal acts against others. It is Jesus's catchall pro-others, anti-sin statement.

To be on point, start by forming operational relationships

Those who demonstrate concern and respect for others will readily develop what we can call an *operational relationship*. This is an interpersonal dynamic that becomes necessary when people on teams are forced to work together to conduct business or create a product or service.

In the business world, these people may not know one another on a personal level, and in some businesses, they may never see one another, because separate departments may be in different buildings or cities. But they must work together for the company to move forward. Many workers depend on others to do their part of a job first, before they can perform their task. The work goes better if they are able to establish at least functional, respectful relationships. If a worker disrespects the workers he or she is dependent on, the business or institution will falter. This basic type of working relationship is to be distinguished from *personal relationships* that may develop later and become far more binding. To some extent, this compares with what is required of parents as they develop relationships with their children from birth to adulthood. At first they don't know each other. They just have to get through the operational part (i.e., distinguishing between yes and no, potty training, etc.). After getting past the "terrible twos," the real relationships develop—for better or for worse. Okay, so maybe I reached for that one, but you get the point.

The person on point will acknowledge interdependence

The point guard always lauds the work of the inside men as well as his shooters. The team works best when he gets some praise in return. Individuals and separate departments work more effectively when they give recognition to fellow workers. Again, think of the family unit. In the best-case scenario, parents must have respect for each other's roles as well as for the position of their children. This benefits the parents as well as the children, especially as the children mature. As children grow older, all family members profit when each shows respect for the other's varying positions in life. Those teen years can be tough, but mutual respect helps soothe the pain for parents and teens. It is certainly easy to relate this concept to business and organizational realms. Everyone gains when each acknowledges the worth of the other's roles and contributions.

The point person utilizes the power of humility

This is part of the model Jesus gave us in his definition of the *serving leader*: if you want to be first, you must consider other people's needs, even before your own. It is what Paul called for when he spoke of "building up" one another (1 Thessalonians 5:11). This requires humility on the part of the one giving the encouragement. Standard wisdom says that humanity is the pinnacle of God's creation. Knowing this, humility comes hard for most of us—well, all of us. But it is one of the most primary elements needed in creating an environment in which a successful team, program or relationship can grow.

Humility is not to be confused with self-degradation, which leads to depression, nor the false humility of the aw-shucks-it-was-nuthin variety. Humility involves consciously sacrificing one's ego or personal desires for the benefit of another. This building-up process is always meaningful, but it is particularly relevant when the other person has a need. At one time or another, we all need building up. A point guard will encourage someone who isn't playing well, and so will a point person who is seeking to influence Life-Team members.

Humility helps an operational relationship to develop into something more personal as well. Successful family, business, political, cultural, and spiritual dynamics often start with operational relationships. These cannot grow or be sustained without some give and take, a sacrificing of egos. If one party disrupts the balance by always claiming to be right or seeks to seize control in too many situations, the union will weaken or crumble. The same occurs if someone places himself above others by constantly blaming or criticizing. Humility creates openness and is inclusive, but conceit erects a fence that is exclusive and shuts out. Humility in one's approach will frame corrective criticism in a more acceptable manner. *Arrogance creates dissension and separation, but humility binds together.*

It is easy to see the interconnectedness of the elements just discussed. You have to practice being others-oriented to begin to have more than just operational relationships. It is impossible even to work together minus this initial functional connection. An assembly line will not function well without each person on the line working smoothly. There would be no good pick and rolls in basketball, no successful double plays in baseball, and no good service at a restaurant without the component parts respecting the interdependence of the whole operation.

Think of the various entities that must work together to get a dinner to your table at a restaurant. The meats and vegetables must be ordered by the owner and delivered in a timely manner. The customers' orders must be submitted to the kitchen properly. One order has onions; the other doesn't. One customer wants the meat rare, and the next wants it medium-well. Various cooks may produce a part of each order. If the cooks are slow, or if the server does not pick up the order when it is ready to leave the kitchen, the customer will not have a good experience. Likewise, if the point guard doesn't pass the ball, no one is happy. He is the ultimate servant.

Communicate with humility

Next needed is a reasonable level of healthy communication to fulfill most simple tasks, and all of the complex ones. Communication with humility means that one person listens to the thoughts and concerns of another in addition to expressing his own opinions. Issues are settled in a humane manner when humility is present.

This type of communication raises the likelihood of *cooperative effectiveness* among the team. What happens is that each person is more likely to applaud the success and contributions of the other team members. Players on highly functional athletic teams will have even those on the bench at any given moment wildly cheering the accomplishments of those in the action. On the other hand, on dysfunctional teams the guys on the sidelines are hoping for their teammates to fail so that they can get in the game.

When unselfishness prevails, teams solidify. They thus validate the entire process by respecting one another's roles and showing high regard for what is being, or has been, accomplished. This respectful phenomenon is often demonstrated in athletics, when teammates of days long gone by keep in touch and speak in glowing terms about one another and their teams. It is not limited to athletics, of course. It is interesting to listen to veteran military men, firefighters, policemen, and even institutional leaders relate tales acknowledging when interdependence in their particular professional environments led to moments of success and victory.

Note how the *internal characteristics* described in the first wheel generate the *external proof* exhibited by the integrated teammate who wants to influence his Life-Teams. Passion for the mission along with preparation, enthusiasm, patience, and persistence are validated by the chain of activity that provides tangible evidence of those qualities. This second wheel is cultivated after establishing the initial internal wheel. But there is much more to our Four-Step System as the next chapter uncovers.

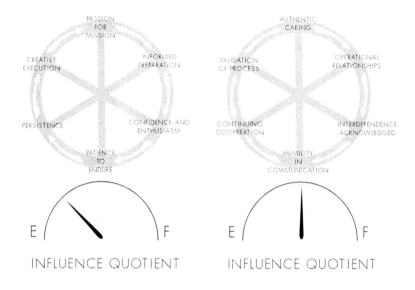

INFLUENCE QUOTIENT INFLUENCE QUOTIENT

STUDY

1. What have you considered to be the most important ingredient in leadership and why? Is it possible to separate this ingredient from several other factors in your thinking? How do you rate your ability to be influential at the present time?

2. Have you found something in your life you are passionate about and is of service to others? Can you think of something exciting outside your professional life (current or future) that would help others?

3. How do you rate yourself on the enthusiasm scale? Why do enthusiastic people tend to draw others to them?

4. Think of how a lack of humility can limit good communication with others. How would this affect one's ability to form good relationships?

5. Review the first two circles shown in this chapter and analyze how each depends on the other to be authentic. What more is needed in the next wheels?

CHAPTER THREE

INCREASING YOUR INFLUENCE QUOTIENT

As influence increases, more is required

The point guard or point person cannot be effective without a measure of raw leadership skill. But we need to go one step at a time. Regardless of our roles on our various Life-Teams, we want to be influential at some level—that is, no normal person prefers to be perpetually ignored. Embracing the methods of successful point guards, as illustrated in our Four-Step System, will help you grow naturally as a leader. Our Life-Teams often include people who need to be mentored. By acquiring the characteristics of the first two wheels and moving forward to the third and fourth wheels, you will see how you can influence others in a good way. Seek to be that kind of person!

Contribute to a positive team environment

Again, we can assume that everyone prefers to be on an effective team. No one likes to see the "L" sign flashed at the mention of his name. While it is not necessary or possible for every endeavor to succeed, if a point person can keep the overall environment positive, the team will survive the ups and downs and be in a better position to win. Once the elements found in the first and second wheels are in place and functioning, it becomes easier to develop and maintain a *positive environment* in which others want to work and are willing to share their efforts and their lives. A good environment will materialize naturally and even add to the caring evidenced when the second wheel is activated. The third wheel follows naturally from the attitudes developed in the wheels that precede it and it surpasses them. All the wheels we will discuss are tightly connected.

Adding the elements of the third wheel

A properly *integrated* person, who has come as far as the second wheel in his growth, contributes to a good working *environment* as a good role player or an emerging leader. He seeks to know his associates' personal contexts and helps them improve their *performance* through attention to detail and proper *mentoring* when appropriate. When able to do so, a good influencer offers his teammates the opportunity to *share a measure of authority* and gives *affirmation* for the good work they do as well as for the people they are becoming. All this perpetuates and fortifies the *positive environment* that generates movement in the third wheel, as shown in the following diagram.

POSITIVE
ENVIRONMENT
WITH
INTEGRITY

AFFIRMATION FOR
JOB WELL DONE

CONTEXT OF
INDIVIDUALS

SHARE
AUTHORITY

IMPROVE THE
PERFORMANCE

MENTORING
PROBLEM
SOLVING

The dynamics of the third wheel

In the overall environment of the team or workplace, all the people will be in the same general milieu—in the business, the church, the family or the institution. Everyone functions better when his or her general environment is good, of course. However, each individual has personal issues, and we refer to that as *personal context*.

This personal context refers to everything that is unique to someone at any given time. It involves factors such as health, family problems, financial questions, and whatever weighs upon that person's mind and may affect that person's attitudes and conduct. In basketball the point guard needs to know when a teammate is having personal or physical issues that may affect that teammate's performance. The point guard knows to expect less of teammates who have such issues if he cannot help resolve them.

If he doesn't know teammates and their personal backgrounds well, the point person will find himself on the outside, looking through an opaque window when he attempts to identify a teammate with a problem. This kind of awareness can only come after concern for and communication with teammates have been established and nurtured. This means that an effective point person goes beyond the *operational relationships* defined in the previous wheel and encourages an environment in which people feel free to form more *personal relationships*. This should not be underestimated in developing a productive team. In sports we call it team chemistry. At home it is called a happy family.

There are many reasons for someone's poor performance or bad day that can be addressed calmly. Fear, lack of support, or guilt may be the issue at any given time for a teammate, friend, or worker. A point person may be able to understand such issues and help a teammate through a situation before those issues become bigger—if he or she has taken the time to get to know his or her teammate well enough. Awareness of the importance of understanding individual contexts is integral to team morale and ultimate success. People who develop this awareness are a step closer to influencing and perhaps leading others effectively.

The point person works to improve the performance of the team

Whether they admit it or not, most people want to get better at the things they do that are important to them. If you can help a person perform better in a reasonably positive manner, that person will *listen*—whether in basketball or any other task. Getting someone to listen is the first order of business for a teacher, coach, mentor, or leader. When a coach or teammate on point can show a player how to execute more efficiently, or show him an offensive or defensive movement that will improve his game, that player will try it. And if it works, he will return for future guidance. The greatest golfers in the world seek the advice of swing and putting coaches in the hope of honing their skills. Even when Tiger Woods was on top of his game, he sought more coaching. Some say he sought too much. But his passion was to be the best golfer ever. Once coaches or leaders prove to be effective, people will seek them out and follow them, no matter whether their expertise is golf, basketball, construction, politics, project planning, or any other undertaking.

It is not enough to be simply a motivator who gets someone to try harder. That helps, but it doesn't last. There will come a day when the motivator will run out of speeches like "Win one for the Gipper" or emotional buttons to push. Getting people to listen is the first step. Getting them to try is the next step. In the end, positive results have to manifest themselves within a reasonable time if you want to maintain your audience, but mentoring, at least for the moment, is a positive step to becoming influential.

A point person pays attention to details

One big difference between good point guards and great ones is attention to detail. While exhibiting this attention to detail, however, they must also keep the process alive and interesting. They can't help a player or a worker to do better if they do not pay attention to the little things. If they are not doing the big things well, they probably should not be on the team in the first place. You can't build anything of lasting value on a bad foundation. For example, when they examined the Titanic, they found that it sank for lack of attention to detail. Engineers installed bolts that were smaller than specified for the hull, thinking a small item like that would be of little consequence. In his book *How NASA Builds Teams*, Robert Pellerin explains the initial failure of the Titanic and that of the $1.7 billion Hubble space telescope. After the Hubble space telescope had been written off as a colossal government failure, Pellerin's unauthorized continual pursuit of a solution to the problem led him to identify and remove a small speck from the giant mirror, an action that led to the revival of the venture. The minute imperfection had been magnified as it was beamed into space. Overlooked minutiae brought down the spacecraft *Challenger* and caused the crashes of various commercial airplanes in recent history as well.[2]

For golfers, one can only imagine the fine points a coach has to make to help players such as Tiger Woods and Phil Mickelson improve their swings. They have to be better than "Keep your eye on the ball, Tiger!" or "Keep your head still, Phil!" That last one has a certain ring to it, though. In line with that, it is amazing to realize the little things that NBA players must learn in order to play a higher level of basketball than they played in college or high school, no matter how high they were drafted. Most people would disagree, thinking that the college game is superior, but that is because the fan cannot see the details going on in close quarters. Virtually no player comes into the NBA with the ability to play NBA-level defense. It takes time to learn how to defend the best players in the world. A central value to having a mix of veteran and younger players on an NBA team is that the veterans can teach what seem to be minor

2   Pellerin, Charles. *How NASA Builds Teams*. Hoboken: Wiley and Sons, 2009, 8–10.

techniques to the younger players, often quite better than many of the coaches can.

Once again, golf offers a good example. If you want to improve your score in the game of golf, you should practice putting. The game is designed for two putts per hole but only one drive. Yet, most amateur golfers spend much more time practicing drives than they spend on the putting green. The putter is the most used club in the bag, but not the most practiced one. You will not use any club, other than the putter, thirty or more times per round. Driving the ball is the big stuff. Good putting is in the details—the little things—and that's where champions excel.

A point person takes time to mentor

People who mentor can contribute immensely to the well-being of others, but much depends on the mentor's ability to communicate. That includes learning to read body language and, most importantly, listening, which is one of the first steps you must take to show that you care for someone. Sustaining your growth as an influential point person and as an effective leader may well depend on that one basic ability. Too many people make the mistake of trying to be an advisor/counselor/critic before taking time to listen. Famous championship football coach Tony Dungy has written an excellent, down-to-earth book that is worthy of study on the value of mentoring entitled, *The Mentor Leader*. He bases his mentorship program on a seven-step process called, The Seven E's. Dungy's seven points are: "engage, educate, equip, encourage, empower, energize, and elevate others." The rest of the system is self-explanatory, but note that the first E is to engage.

In the beginning Dungy states that a mentor must engage himself through effective communication, which involves spending time empathizing with the one being mentored. He writes, "It is impossible to mentor from a distance. Without engagement you cannot lead effectively."[3] Of course, engagement begins with demonstrated caring and is facilitated by effective communication. To "engage" means "to become involved" or "to attract and hold fast," according to dictionary.com. This indicates a personal, caring act takes place, as opposed to lecturing or pontificating. Engaging draws others to you, but more importantly it draws you to others. When mentoring is done well, people follow. And we call a person whom others follow "one who is influencing or leading."

A person on point will help resolve problems quickly

The team builder will be dedicated to becoming a quick problem solver. In doing so, the elements of concern for others and the ability to communicate effectively again become big factors. Do not let problems turn into disasters. "Don't let the sun go down on your wrath" is a good biblical exhortation (Ephesians 4:26). Teams that are known to have good chemistry are ones that settle conflicts quickly. Especially when a situation requires a stern reprimand, it is best not to have too much carryover time before resolving the conflict. When you wait to resolve a problem, you extend and magnify it. Unresolved issues that carry on for days are destructive.

On the other hand, *being patient* to avoid overreacting is an important attribute to cultivate as well. One of the best bits of advice I received in all my years of coaching came from my first general

---

3 Dungy, Tony. *The Mentor Leader*. Carol Stream, IL: Tyndale House, 2010, 166.

manager, the late Ray Patterson of the Houston Rockets. He was a masterful GM, who engineered championships with the Milwaukee Bucks and the Rockets. During my first year as a head NBA coach, he gave me this simple admonition: "Remember this. Whatever happens, don't overreact." When I follow that counsel, it pays off. When I do not follow that advice, I am the one who generally pays.

The point person will share authority

Once in charge, to some degree, those who exercise good leadership skills understand the value of promoting some level of ownership in the program by sharing authority with team members when appropriate. This takes a bit of humility on the part of those who want to be leaders, but that can be developed over time. It ultimately requires sacrificing personal ego while expanding that of others—always a good plan if done with competent people. The great Marquette University basketball coach Al McGuire used to tell his trusted assistants that he didn't want to hear about the little problems. It was up to them to settle those brushfires. If it became a $5,000 problem, they should bring it to him. In sports a good leader has relative "control of the locker room," thus freeing up the coach for the bigger issues. In Exodus 18:21–23, Moses got some similar advice from his father-in-law when he told him to "select capable men from all the people—men who fear God, trustworthy men who hate dishonest gain—and appoint them as officials over thousands, hundreds, fifties, and tens. Have them serve as judges for the people at all times, but have them bring every difficult case to you; the simple cases they can decide themselves. That will make your load lighter, because they will share it with you."

Again, there will be levels of influence and leadership in a larger group of people, as suggested in the story of Moses. Good leaders start others on the path to leadership by giving them limited authority. They expand that authority as it is earned and as one's Influence Quotient increases. The wise person will take his assignment of authority seriously and build on it. Sharing authority over smaller things is not insignificant, keeping in mind the stories of the *Titanic* and the Hubble space telescope mission. Minor breakdowns lead to major ones. As people handle the smaller things well, they can move up to deal with the more significant tasks. Ultimately, this can grow into having an increased level of input in larger issues.

A point person gives credit freely

Mature leaders are good at sharing credit, and a large part of that is accomplished by offering affirmation for a job well done. At the beginning that can be hard to do. A person given responsibility for the first time can become jealous for his position. In the worst cases, some lord their newfound authority over the people now beneath them. Others are afraid to give praise or credit for fear of losing their place. But team building thrives when leaders are quick to show recognition and give praise, even for what seem to be relatively minor items. Try to remember how you got to where you are when you're in a higher position. Your workers and my players want to know two things: "What do you want me to do? And how do you think I am doing?" You must give them confidence in the overall vision and their part in it, along with a degree of ownership in the ongoing progress of the mission when they earn it. Affirmations are almost as meaningful when they come from a peer who seeks to influence the program for good as they are when they come from the actual leader.

A part of that acknowledgement may come in the form of raises and bonuses when a leader is in position to authorize them, but more subtle rewards of encouragement go as far in the short run. Again, a compliment from a team member can be a huge lift, and it costs little to give. What I am saying is that we learn early in life that small things matter; a "smiley face" on our school tests or homework is a good thing. Something that ends up under a magnet on the refrigerator has value to youngsters. Rewards don't have to be valuable intrinsically, but they have to *be of some value at the time to that person.* The value may fade, but the concept doesn't. In the end, promotions and raises are required in business. However, it is truly comical to see NBA players compete so much harder for $100 in a practice shooting game than in one that is just a drill. That $100 bill represents a "smiley face" to them, as well as a victory. And Ben Franklin does seem to wear a bit of a grin himself. Considering all the millions many NBA players are paid, it is hilarious to see one jumping around when he beats his peers in a shooting game, holding the money up and looking as proud as a medal-winning Olympian waving his country's flag. All that is missing is the National Anthem. Some $100 bills are apparently worth more than others.

A review of the previous wheels presented in Chapter 2 shows that leadership plays a major role in team building, but is only a part of it. Leadership is not a stand-alone characteristic. It is an important part of the process of team building and increases as one develops his Influence Quotient and the team improves. The wheels offer a simple illustration of how teammates can benefit their Life-Teams as they work to master the connective parts of the process in a sequential and logical manner. Growth emerges from the inside, from the heart of a person or organization, focused on purposeful mission planning and proper attitudinal development. The inner qualities that are demonstrated outwardly in a consistent manner make team members more comfortable in an *environment* that encourages growth and shares authority while providing personal satisfaction.

Still, there is much more to consider as we move toward the establishment of a great Life-Team vehicle and the forming of lasting relationships. How does that happen? You'll see in the next chapter, where we talk about the fourth wheel. Examine the three wheels pictured below to see how the progression works.

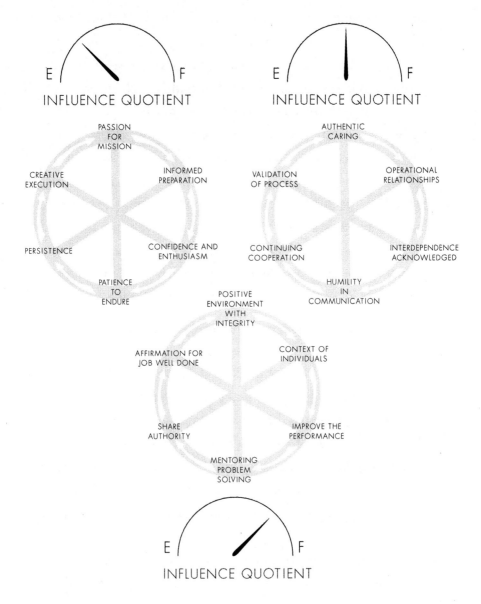

STUDY

1. Describe the difference between one's environment and one's personal context.

2. Describe how the lack of attention to detail can ruin the performance of a worker and a business. Think especially about the business you are in or wish to be in the future. How about in the family?

3. How important is the role of a mentor in someone's life? Is there an obligation for mature people to be willing to mentor?

4. How does sharing authority lend a sense of ownership in a group or business? How will it affect the working environment?

5. Now review the first three wheels and try to think of what is missing in order to effect greater team building. Would this be enough at this point to have a decent team?

CHAPTER FOUR

BUILDING UP OTHERS IS LIFE-TEAM WORK

A good point guard majors in building up others:

The other four players always look to the point guard for cues. Point guards have the ball much of the time on offense, and are out front on defense. Their body language, demeanor, and overall attitude can be infectious—for good or for bad. For this reason, the great point persons will be encouragers. Encouragement is a good, infectious quality. Of course, everything that happens on the court, or in life, is not okay. Positive responses are not always appropriate. Providing trophies for everyone hasn't worked out all that well in youth sports, for instance. Good mentoring also requires the identification and correction of mistakes. But a point person's overall approach should have an aura of positivism mixed with realism that is necessary when breakdowns need to be addressed. Perhaps the lowly battery offers a good metaphor. To make things work, a battery must have both a positive and a negative element. Perhaps what we are looking for here is "positive negativism"? We need both kinds of input.

We all should be encouragers as leaders or role players on our various teams, but always in an appropriate context. We should be encouragers when it is time to encourage and applauders when it is time to applaud. But to offer giddy cheers like a pom-pom girl, regardless of performance quality, will take away from those times the team player really deserves recognition for a job well done. And it will give mixed signals to one who needs correction along with a measure of encouragement.

Fulfilling our mission to build up others energizes our Life-Teams. We have previously alluded to the value of encouragement in terms of showing enthusiasm, but I refer here to *affirmation-plus*— affirmation combined with enthusiasm. An incredible chain reaction follows an unselfish act of encouragement, even if we don't feel like giving it at that moment. A continuous enthusiastic atmosphere drives a team to new heights.

Why the fourth wheel?

With the first three wheels intact, it would seem we are well on our way to developing a successful Life-Team. Anyone who has followed the first three wheels has built up a cachet as an influential team member by this point. Leaders are now doing a good job and role players are improving. Their Influence Quotients rise as they gain confidence in their ability to lead. A basketball team following the first three wheels wins a whole lot of games. *But it won't be a champion team at this point.* Neither will a corporation, a church, an institution, or a family. There is still something lacking. The Influence Quotient tank is not yet full.

Let's assess the chain reaction shown in the fourth wheel as a team pursues its mission. Having set up an environment that is healthy and on track based on the previous wheels, we look to the ultimate aim of our Life-Teams: relationships. Team members must seek to *build up* others on the team, and eliminate the mistrust that selfishness creates. Team members must earn *trust* by performing consistently in a manner that is true to the overall mission. Then trust will blossom into stronger, more personal *loyalty*. When loyalty is nurtured and sustained, a deeper sentiment often emerges: *affection* or even *love*. Such affection, or love, creates a unified environment. And *unity* is the most central element for *enduring relationships*. This is defined best by the phrase in the marriage ceremony, "the two will become one." Ongoing encouragement and building up perpetuates the momentum in the resulting wholesome environment.

Scriptural admonitions relative to the fourth wheel:

Romans 15:2 reads, "Each of us should please his neighbor to build him up." We are implored in 1 Thessalonians 5:11 to "encourage one another and build each other up." Building up compounds trust; tearing another down causes resentment. That is why we need to find a time to offer encouragement fairly soon after we have had to make corrections. *If you are not building up, you are contributing to tearing down* in the sense that anyone who is not being fed is starving. If you have food to give and withhold it, people starve. There is no "zero" in either of these relational transactions. You help when needed, or you do harm by doing nothing. It is difficult to trust someone who is always negative toward you, but the world loves an honest encourager.

Please close your eyes and visualize in the following personal experiment:

1. Think of someone in your past who has torn you down by being overly critical, doubtful, or hateful. Visualize the face of that person and hold it in your mind for thirty seconds.

2. Now picture in your mind someone who has encouraged you or supported you in a time of need. Give that image thirty seconds as well. It is important to visualize the face involved.

3. Notice the difference in the feeling you had in those two instances. I am guessing that your body seemed to *shrink* when you remembered the negative experience, and to *expand* when you remembered the positive. Your face probably reflected the difference between those two moments as well. Which one do you trust?

You and your team cannot excel if you and your teammates do not build one another up. When you do this, you unleash an abundance of good feelings. Paul calls giving encouragement one of the gifts of the Spirit in Romans 12:6–8. This is a role we all can fill, at least to some degree. Not everyone can teach, or govern, or donate large sums of money, but we can all serve in some way. We can all be encouragers. It only costs a little ego.

To build trust a point person must be consistent

The teammates of a good point guard know that if they work to become open, he will send the ball to the right place. They develop an even deeper trust in him because of his consistency in doing that game after game. Trust involves placing reliance on the integrity of a person, concept, or thing. Consistency in performance promotes an increasing trust in the integrity of all things: friends, teammates, brakes, good government, and so forth. Take bridges, for example. We pass over many of them in the process of driving to work, shopping, or vacationing. Occasionally, we hear of a big bridge collapsing while cars and trucks were on it, resulting in a number of deaths and injuries. For a while after hearing such news, we to want to get off a bridge as quickly as possible. That's human nature. Admit it. You have lost a bit of the trust you once had in bridges.

Similarly, when we board an airplane, most of us give little thought to the possibility of a breakdown, though many of us pray for God to bless the flight, just in case. Nonetheless, after two or three passenger planes crash in short succession, those thoughts and prayers are much more prevalent and urgent than usual. This simply illustrates that trust comes through consistency, and even though it takes time and experience for it to develop, it can be broken rather abruptly.

A good point person will gain loyalty—try *Ubuntu*

Loyalty is deeper than trust. Loyalty connotes devotion and allegiance to a person, cause, or concept. Loyalty adds sentiment to trust. To illustrate, let us consider the Boston Celtics of 2007–08. The Celtics were down and thought to be out after the 2007 season. Rumors were flying that Coach Doc Rivers would not survive to Christmas on the bench if they did not get off to a good start. But they made a pair of key acquisitions during the off-season with two older players, Kevin Garnett and Ray Allen. They joined the Celtics' all-star Paul Pierce, and the team's mix of youth and other older, experienced role players. Most "experts" thought they had improved themselves as a team but did not consider them winning a championship, largely because they were too old. But they confounded the forecasters by putting together a championship season, winning the NBA rings in that 2007–08 season. Again, the same experts were undaunted and predicted the Celtics might have enough for that one final shot but would not be able to repeat the process in 2008–09. Well, they were right technically, but not completely.

The Celtics did not get back to the finals in 2008–09, but they did have another excellent year. Then, with essentially the same team in 2009–10, the Celtics continued to play well, but they were regarded no better than the third-best team in the Eastern Conference. Nonetheless, they withstood the favored Cleveland Cavaliers and LeBron James, who had the best record in the league that year, as well as the Orlando Magic and all-star center Dwight "Superman"

Howard. With practically the same contingent as in 2008, the Celtics competed fiercely in the finals before finally bowing to the heavily favored defending champions, the Los Angeles Lakers. You may know all this, but what you probably do not know is the role *Ubuntu* may have played. *Ubuntu* is a concept for life that Bishop Desmond Tutu developed and expressed in his book *Believe*.[4] I will paraphrase in brief some of the main points:

1. One who has *Ubuntu* will be friendly to and caring of others.

2. He will use his strength on behalf of others and will never take advantage of them.

3. The finest picture of man is when he can put *we over me*— when he can subject himself in service to others for the good of the whole—that is, the team, group or family.

4. He explains how the spirit of *Ubuntu* enabled his people to forgive those in South Africa who had committed atrocities against the native South African people during the apartheid era, and how it led to successful unification of the nation.

Doc Rivers, his staff, and players read *Believe* before the start of the 2007–08 season. The Celtics accepted *Ubuntu* as a way of life for their team. It became their mission to relate that way to one another, and to let that lead them to become the best they could be. They talked of it often and repeated the term *Ubuntu* in practice, games and when they broke from huddles.

---

4   Tutu, Bishop Desmond, *Believe*. Boulder, CO: Philips, 2007.

Fear that you are not talented enough to be on the point?

Talent is overrated. You know this is true. The Celtics' 2010 achievement was, perhaps, as big an accomplishment as the title run. Either Cleveland or Orlando was supposed to be playing the Lakers for that NBA championship, but certainly not the Celtics. Those teams had great talent, but did not have as much *Ubuntu* as the Celtics. Talent is only one element in determining success. There are many talented people incarcerated in the prisons of the world—talented people who misused their talents, or used the wrong ones. The 2009–10 Celtics played with an intensity and unselfishness that carried them, as the oldest team in the league, to victory in 2007–08 and to the finals again two years later. Amazingly the same core was still effective in the 2011–12 season, pushing the favored Heat to seven games in the Conference finals. That is the power of *Ubuntu*.

In the process, the Celtics developed a genuine trust and love for one another. Through that love came a unity that made the sum of the team greater than its individual parts, ages notwithstanding. The team continued to be successful, due largely to relationships established in the *Ubuntu* environment. And the Celtics are not an isolated case. We will go a little further with other sports examples, and then relate all this to the spiritual domain. The fourth wheel is the last of the necessary wheels required for movement in dynamic team building. It illustrates the connective characteristics of the ultimate goal of Life-Teams: lasting relationships.

The 1977 Portland Trailblazers

Let us consider another sports-related bit of evidence of this dynamic. Late in 2010, Maurice Lucas, a great former NBA player, died after enduring a tough battle with cancer. Big Luke, or Mo, was a great competitor and was probably the most skilled basketball player in NBA annals who also had the role of "enforcer" on the team. This type of player traditionally has limited overall basketball skills, but not big Luke. He played alongside Bill Walton, a noted peacemaker with even greater skills. The two led an excellent Portland Trailblazers crew of complementary players to the NBA title in 1977 under Hall of Fame coach Jack Ramsay. At the time of his death, Big Luke was an assistant coach with the Blazers. In writing a free-flowing eulogy of Big Luke, Peter Vescey, the iconic sportswriter for *The New York Post,* gave great insight into the inner workings of that outstanding championship team, and into Maurice Lucas as a person. The following are excerpts of Vescey's sensitive article that reveal some teammates' recollections of Lucas and that great season:[5]

> "Johnny Davis was 20 when the Blazers drafted him in
> 1976, the league's youngest player that season. Luke sat
> him down and explained the facts of NBA life. His interest
> in the newcomer and persistent positive approach grab
> Davis to this day. Davis reminisced, 'He would've given
> me the shirt off his back. What he did give me was confi-
> dence. He was forever pumping me up. He told me I was
> faster than anyone in the league, so to use that speed to
> blow by people and don't worry about anything else. He
> told me all season to stay ready. When Dave [Twardzik]
> got hurt in the Denver play-off series and I was put into

---

5   Vescey, Peter. "Teammates recall Lucas' eternal friendship". *New York Post*, Nov. 2, 2010.

the starting lineup, he met me at the locker room door and said, 'This is what you've been waiting for, Rookie. This is going to be your coming out party!'

"Davis said he had a good game and the Blazers won. Late in the fourth quarter, a Denver player was shooting a free throw and Luke had inside position. Davis was on the same side with a Nugget between them. Luke reached behind the guy and tapped me, smiled, and winked, as if to say, 'I told you this would be your coming out party.' I'll never forget that or what he did for me. Our team's chemistry and camaraderie were forever. We froze that [championship] moment and it only belongs to us. We cared about each other. He cared about us. We cared about him. His friendship was unconditional. I texted him regularly. A week or so ago he didn't text back. I knew that couldn't be good."

It was a wonderful tribute to Maurice that went on for several pages with the recollections of various teammates and opposing players and coaches. One cannot help but look at the brief summary reprinted here and relate some of the key words and actions to the very things we have noted. This was a man "on point." Luke was someone who committed to the mission and was prepared mentally and physically. He cared deeply for his teammates and was an *encourager who built up others*. He knew his role and fulfilled it gladly. He created an environment of support and loyalty, and the love flowed on that team into a giant pool of unity. The relationships that resulted were forever. Luke was a great point person.

The 2010 Texas Rangers

I have lived in the Dallas area since 2000 and during those years the Rangers did very little to capture the imagination of North Texas or the Metroplex of Dallas/Ft. Worth—that is, not until the summer of 2010. They started out of the gates fast and never let up, winning the division easily. And they did it with a team that was in bankruptcy and seeking a new owner at the start of the season, along with some other issues that did not bode well for the summer. Still, many didn't have a lot of hope that they would prevail in the play-offs because they had not done it before. And then there were always the Yankees to have to deal with. But they went all the way to the World Series before finally succumbing to the Giants. Nevertheless, eliminating the Yankees was like winning the World Series for this franchise. They had never had success against this top franchise in all of baseball. Their victory against the Yankees in the sixth game of the play-offs that got them to the World Series was the biggest win in franchise history. In postgame interviews Josh Hamilton, the league MVP, and fellow slugger Nelson Cruz gave honor to God first and then talked of how much love they had for their teammates. The broadcasters talked at length about the unity of the team. You can try to do it another way, but this is the right way. This was a true *we-over-me* team. It was a team that stayed on course toward its mission while developing trust and loyalty in the ranks. This grew into a love that brought the team together in unity of spirit and purpose. There is no greater feeling for a team. Relationships that endure for a lifetime result from this degree of camaraderie. And the core of that same team made a second trip to the World Series the following year.

The 2011 Dallas Mavericks

Again, championships don't just happen. There is a systematic route to get to the kind of leadership and environment that produces them. It happens in all sports, and it happens in corporate and institutional life as well. When the 2011 season began, the Mavericks were not considered by any of the experts to be one of the top six teams in the league; they were seen as a nonthreat in the championship. The team was the oldest in the league, and although they had excellent seasons throughout the first decade of the new century, they faltered in the finals of 2006 to Miami and had been able to win only one postseason round since. They were billed as the one-and-out-boys by many of the fans in the city. After a great start at 24–5, they lost a key player for the rest of the season because of an injury, their number-two scoring starter, Caron Butler. Soon after this loss, their star, Dirk Nowitzki, missed nine games because of a knee injury. The team lost seven of those games. All seemed lost for yet another season as far as any play-off success was concerned.

However, the team was noted for wonderful camaraderie and for teammates' ability to set aside individual accomplishments for the good of the team. The 2011 team had added a strong defensive presence in center Tyson Chandler. He was an enthusiastic, charismatic locker-room leader as well. The entire team had a strong commitment to a mission of winning the championship. All the key returning players were in their thirties, led by the great point guard Jason Kidd, aged thirty-eight. Another charismatic leader, he knew he did not have many opportunities left in his career to win a ring. Dirk would turn thirty-three at the end of the season, and Jason Terry had already hit that milestone. All three players were dedicated to the task of winning a championship, regardless of injuries and setbacks. Upon Dirk's return after an injury, the Mavericks bounced back to put together a string of nineteen wins in twenty-one games, but then they seemed to wear down and bottom out as the season came to an end in early April. They managed to win their last five regular season games against weak, nonplay-off opponents. In fact, during the closing six weeks of the season, they failed to beat any play-off-bound team, winning only against those who would be watching from the sidelines.

Their first-round opponent, Portland, was perceived to be a bad draw for the Mavs and most predicted the Blazers would beat them, even though the Mavericks had the better record. It looked even worse when the Mavs gave up a 23-point lead in the second half to lose game four in Portland. That loss tied the series at 2–2. However, they bounced back to win the next two games, but their reward was to play against the two-time defending NBA champion Lakers, who were seeking a second three-peat in the Kobe Bryant era. The Mavs shocked the basketball world by not only winning, but also by sweeping the series 4–0, while overwhelming the hapless Lakers in game four with the score of 122–86—and the game wasn't that close. Next up were the young legs and guns from Oklahoma City, an outstanding, youthful team who many believed would run the aging Mavs off the court. However, once again, the experts underestimated the resolve and the team play of Dallas. Not only did they beat the Thunder four games to one, they did it by averaging more than 105 points per game.

Then the true test came. As usual, the doubters ruled the airwaves, because the opponent would be the "dream team," the Miami Heat. The Heat still had Dwayne Wade, the Mavericks' nemesis from the play-off finals of 2006, plus a lot more. Wade was still young and strong with even more experience. But beyond that, the Heat had loaded up with what many thought from the start of the season would surely be the next champion for the upcoming season and for many years to follow. LeBron James, the player generally considered one of the two best players in the game at that time, had been added as a free agent during the summer. He had deserted his hometown Cleveland team and made the well-publicized "decision" on national television to "take my talents to South Beach." In addition, the Toronto all-star Chris Bosh had signed on to come along with LeBron. It appeared to be a lay-down hand for the title, initially. And by the time the Heat faced the Mavericks, few gave the older Mavs any more than a long-shot chance to win. Interestingly, they said that the only hope the Mavs had was that they played a strong team-oriented game, but the Heat had the stars, and the traditional NBA axiom has been that "stars win championships."

It turned out that both schools of thought proved to be correct. Team play, togetherness, and total commitment did win the title. But so did the "stars" who just happened to be wearing Mavs uniforms and were central to that team's efforts. Dirk Nowitzki was unanimously named the MVP of the series. He and Jason Terry, who scored twenty-six points in the final game, showed why they were among the top five fourth-quarter scorers in the NBA during the regular season. They demonstrated how championship players and teams finish games. Jason Kidd, Tyson Chandler, Shawn Marion, and J. J. Barea were other great role-playing contributors who allowed Dirk and Terry to be the stars. On the other hand, the inability of the Heat to close out a game was emphasized in game two at Miami, the real turning point in the series. The Heat led by fifteen points with four minutes remaining, but the Mavs clawed their way back into the game to overcome that deficit and give the Mavs the home-court advantage, because the next three games were to be played in Dallas. This game set a trend in which the Mavericks would win by closing out fourth quarters better than the Heat.

The Mavs lost game three at home as their late rally fell short, and the experts went right back to preferring the odds for a Heat victory in the series. But Dallas came from behind to win game four and then ran away with relatively easy wins in game five and game six by dominating the fourth quarter. There was a picture of Dirk giving Jason Terry an extended hug after that final game that says more than words can about the bond that these players shared through this great championship run. They and their teammates formed lifetime relationships through their inspiring team performance.

Relationships like those noted above grow out of unity, but they cannot happen or last if someone insists on putting individuality ahead of unity. Those who cannot put "we over me" in their hearts will not be a lasting part of the unity and the resulting relationships. Even if they were on the team as strong statistical contributors, they would never enjoy the fullness of that experience. What a shame to grab something for yourself, only to guarantee through that selfish act that you will not receive it. He that seeks to put himself first will be the least of all. That holds true individually and in relationships as well.

I am speculating that it is far from coincidental that the Miami Heat put together an exceptional team game to go along with their outstanding stars that propelled them to the NBA title in 2012.

Jesus emphasized unity as a point person

The entire seventeenth chapter of John is dedicated to Jesus's longest recorded prayer and presents solid scriptural verification of my point on unity here. In this chapter Jesus prayed for three entities: himself, his immediate disciples, and those believers who would follow after them. Initially, he prayed for his own mission that was about to come to fulfillment, and then he asked for three things for his immediate disciples: protection, unity (v. 11) and sanctification. Finally, he prayed to the Father on behalf of all of us who would come to believe in him after the disciples—"those who will believe in me through their message" (v. 20). At that point Jesus made a most significant request as it relates to our point here. Remember, this was just before he was arrested, put on trial, and crucified. This is what was on his mind at that crucial time. His prayer to the Father for his future followers was this: "I have given them the glory that you have given me, *that they may be one as we are one, I in them and you in me.* May they be brought to *complete unity* to let the world know that you sent me and have loved them, even as you have loved me" (v. 22, 23). What amazing words! Such is the importance and power of unity. There can be no closer relationship than this. It is the power that has allowed the word of Jesus's redemptive message to be spread throughout the centuries. We will discuss further scriptural proof of all the points described in our wheels in the next chapter.

But what if things still go wrong sometimes?

The system we have described here in the process of constructing the four-wheeled vehicle are similar to the wheels of any vehicle—they can malfunction. There can be leaks or even blowouts. All good things require diligence. We live in a rapidly changing world. Regardless of how well things may be operating with an individual, a team, or an organization, problems will eventually arise, assuming everyone involved is human.

While there will never be a simple answer that can apply to all situations, one method that can be used is to start at the fourth wheel and go backward to find where the chain has broken down. Review the wheels on the following page. For example, when it has become obvious that relationships are not as strong as they need be, one can retrack the route in team building that had provided success. It is quite possible that none of the four wheels is functioning properly—there has been a total blowout. Maybe there is a leak in which people have become careless or egocentric to the point that they are not building one another up. If one goes back through the wheels, the root cause can be found. Leaks may occur at any one of the points. Are team members getting affirmation? Is the breakdown because of a lack of mentoring, or maybe a lack of understanding of the backgrounds of one or several of the team members? Obviously, there can be degrees of lacking in more than one area.

The next step to take would be to start at the very beginning of the mission, just to double-check. Move forward point by point to see if you meet at the same point in the first step, or perhaps there is an even earlier cause for the slowdown. Quite likely, there will be a realization that multiple factors can stand improvement. The expectation should be that once the "potholes"—the root causes—have been identified, solutions can be determined. The points that had once been functioning quite well can hopefully be patched up, and momentum will resume. Each factor tends to feed off the previous one and, in turn, support the next step. When the team gets back to the process of building each other up, it is just a matter of time before trust will be re-established, which leads to the restoration of relationships.

In the next chapter we will examine how various spiritual leaders in the Bible applied the common principles presented in our four wheels to team building. These were people "on point" even before the world had point guards. You will see how the concepts presented are not only sound scripturally but are actually promoted in the Scriptures.

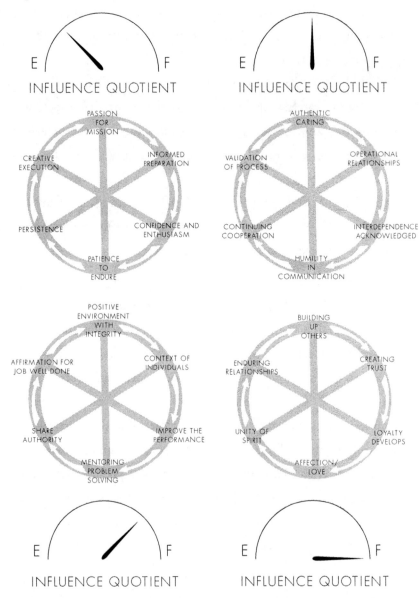

STUDY

1. How do building one another up and selfishness run counter to each other?

2. Explain how failing to build up can contribute to tearing down.

3. How can "we over me" work in the home? In your workplace?

4. Why is talent sometimes overrated? Do you sometimes compare yourself to others instead of seeking to be the best you can be?

5. Review the four wheels that have been described and get a sense of them. Think of how these relate to your experiences and to biblical teachings.

CHAPTER FIVE

SCRIPTURAL EXAMPLES OF PEOPLE ON POINT

There were a lot of point guards in the Bible

While there were no basketballs at that time, there were many biblical leaders who applied the various characteristics that are exhibited by good point guards and go together to form the integrated wheels of team building. Whether one is a Christian or not, it is indisputable that Jesus was a great team builder, so we begin with him. He was the ultimate team man whose prime mission was to do the will of the one who sent him. He started with twelve men, most of whom were simple fishermen with little education. They came from Galilee, which was considered the backwoods, "hillbilly" section of Israel, but the movement he and these men initiated has endured for more than 2000 years.

Jesus's leadership style was that of the serving leader. His theme was, "If you want to be first, you put yourself last." His advice for becoming a leader was to care about others and let them know it by serving them, particularly when serving them fulfilled a need. An oft-cited example is that of washing his disciples' feet on his last night with them. Jesus said, "He that would be the greatest must be the servant of all." In fact, that moment of humble service was a very minor example compared to his life in servitude, climaxed by his crucifixion and resurrection, given for our benefit. Let's review his pattern of leadership in the following pages.

Committed to the mission? Check!

Obviously, Jesus had all of the great qualities noted in our four wheels, demonstrating them throughout his life. He prepared for thirty years before beginning his three-year ministry to fulfill the myriad of prophecies foretold of him. He knew the Scriptures at age twelve to the amazement of the scholars of the day. His patience with sinners and his group of disciples is well documented, as well as his ability to endure opposition and incredible pain and suffering. So dreadful was his immediate future that Luke 22:42 indicates he asked if there might be a Plan B that could be put into effect, but he submitted, saying "not my will, but your will [the Father's plan]." As he envisioned the pain he would have to endure, "His sweat was like drops of blood, falling to the ground," according to Dr. Luke (Luke 22:44). Jesus had a mission to fulfill as the Savior of mankind and was relentless in his dedication to the task given him by the Father.

It is of great significance to consider the type of person Jesus was, as revealed in the various narratives in the Gospels. In his book *The Jesus I Never Knew*, Philip Yancey notes a number of references that give us glimpses of Jesus's humanity.[6] I have found Yancey's book to be of tremendous help in analyzing Jesus as a man. I have leaned on his overall analysis of Jesus's human nature in describing his leadership style and comparing it to that of the point guard.

---

6   Yancey, Philip. *The Jesus I Never Knew*. Grand Rapids: Zondervan, 1995.

At the beginning of Jesus's public ministry, he first selected three men and quickly gathered together the rest of an inner circle of twelve followers who would be with him constantly for three years. After a time, he organized a group of seventy-two followers whom he sent out to spread his "news" and to prepare towns for his arrival. It is quite possible that the original twelve brought in the new initiates, though there is no indication that this was the case. It is an irresistible thought, given that Andrew met Jesus and then brought Peter to him, and that the mission of the twelve and subsequent disciples was to bring people to Jesus. Jesus at one point sent out the original disciples two by two to spread the word and heal. Jesus later sent the seventy-two men on the second of what we now call "mission trips." That team was so successful that even demons submitted to them in Jesus's name.

Exhibited supreme integrity? Check!

Jesus's deeds matched his words. He asked his followers to lower themselves to become servants. Washing his disciples' feet at the last meal was only the tip of the iceberg to his serving leadership. He did far more. He embodied every quality we have noted in defining the characteristics integral to great leadership, team building, and loving relationships. Chapter five of Yancey's book gives an extensive list of Jesus's human characteristics and most are of note as we consider his leadership methods.[7]

1. He was approachable, even to children.

---

7   Ibid. pp. 85–99.

2. He was gregarious, not averse to turning water into fine wine during the wedding feast at Cana at the request of his mother.

3. He had a very serious and disciplined side, enabling him to interpret the Scriptures at the age of twelve, yet he prepared until he was thirty.

4. He said his burden was easy and his yoke was light, but he was demanding, and anything but weak or passive. Details mattered.

5. He was tender, yet tough at the same time. He could heal the sick and afflicted and could calm the storms of life.

6. He was so committed to his purpose emotionally that he overturned the tables in the Temple when he saw how it was being defiled.

7. He was bold and truthful. He called the deceitful and arrogant Pharisees and Sadducees "snakes" to their faces. He spoke of impending judgment, when there would be weeping, wailing and gnashing of teeth.

8. He demonstrated ultimate integrity by living a loving and sinless life, setting a great example for his followers.

9. He set high goals for his followers, but he extended grace and mercy to them when they fell short of those goals.

10. He was a giver of rewards. To his closest followers he gave the power over evil spirits and sickness. To believers he offers eternal life.

Exhibited caring and concern? Check!

We have noted that caring is where a person who leads must prove himself first of all. He must be truly others-oriented. Jesus described himself as the Good Shepherd who knew his sheep and would lay down his life for them. He dramatically revealed his caring for all people, regardless of station in life, throughout the Gospel narratives. He was "moved with compassion" at various times when he saw afflicted people who were sick, blind, or even dead. He wept upon the temporary death of his friend, Lazarus. When he looked over Jerusalem upon his grand entry into the city at the start of his final week in his earthly body, he said he would gladly have gathered everyone under his wing, as a hen might protect her young. He knew his people and he loved them.

Live in the power of humility? Check!

He was born in poverty, and worked as a carpenter. In his last three years he was basically homeless, with "no place to lay his head." He carried no money on him, apparently, but could turn a couple of fish into a feast. He understood well the power of humility, living and preaching it constantly, just as it had been prophesied of him in the Psalms and the Prophets. He chose to ride on a donkey instead of a horse or in chariots on his triumphal entry into Jerusalem. He was able to speak with authority, as no other teacher had, but without arrogance. He explained deep truths with simple stories of everyday life.

He had great self-esteem, but his confidence sprang from his relationship with the Father and never interfered with his humility. In the Garden of Gethsemane, he clearly exhibited his humanity, humility, and dependence on the Father, yielding to the Father's mission for him. Though he had all powers, he chose not to defend himself at his trials, even though he understood he was not only a king, but the king of kings. His constant mantra was that to become strong it was important to admit to one's personal weakness, while depending upon strength from the Father. He expected that of his followers as well. For example, he couldn't fully use Peter until Peter had been "broken" in spirit after learning humility and dependence, but once that was accomplished after Peter's three denials, Jesus charged Peter to "feed my sheep" as his point man.

He could hold a dialogue with the brightest of minds, the scholars of the day, in their language. He could also speak to little children, who wanted to be close to him. But he was most comfortable in the presence of those uneducated fishermen and those perceived to be lower elements on the social ladder: tax collectors, prostitutes, and sinners in general. He was the great physician who came to heal those in need of healing, whether physical or spiritual, but especially the latter. To accomplish this, relationships had to be formed, which could only be done through loving communication.

Provide a good environment and know personal contexts? Check!

He could have stayed aloof and moved from place to place much faster, but he chose to walk with his group close by him at all times. He fostered a great environment in which they could learn all that they would need to know after he had returned to the Father. True, there were occasions when he chose to go off alone, such as the forty days of temptation, and other times when he went off to pray alone. But those occasions were rare. He chose three disciples from the twelve—Peter, James and John—to be his intimates in the inner circle. He allowed them to accompany him to the Mount of Transfiguration and deeper into the Garden of Gethsemane than the rest of the twelve disciples on that last night, when he was betrayed and arrested. Meals are a good time to get to know people more intimately. He took time to eat meals with not only his disciples but all sorts of people. He knew their strengths and weaknesses, who would deny him, who would doubt him, who had a temper, who wanted to sit at his right hand, who would be the best to watch over his mother after his ascension, and who would sell him out. After the resurrection he gathered his eleven remaining disciples together again and spent time with them and others until his ascension.

Shared His authority? Check!

He not only gave his disciples powers during the learning process as they traveled from place to place. In the end he gave all the powers he had to the disciples in terms of performing miracles and forming the framework and leadership of the Church. After teaching and walking with them daily for three years, he left them in charge. He did not abandon them, however. He equipped them and all subsequent believers with the Holy Spirit as guide and counselor. Armed with this power, these men were then able to start a movement that has continued to grow around the world. And that power is still at work today in the hearts of those who believe and follow his teachings as they encourage and lead others.

Gave affirmation to his followers? Check!

He was an encourager, one who gave affirmation to others. He called Peter the Rock long before Peter was anything close to that. In truth,

Peter was oftentimes a rock head, stubborn and aggressive. He praised the faith of the non-Jewish Roman centurion who believed Jesus could heal his Jewish servant by just saying the word, as opposed to making the trip to the centurion's home. Referring to the centurion, Matthew 8:10 reads, "When Jesus heard this, He was astonished and said to those following him, 'I tell you the truth, I have not found anyone in Israel with such great faith.'" He was exceedingly complimentary of the work the seventy-two did on their mission trip. That Jesus was proud of them is recorded in Luke 10:20, in which he said, "Do not rejoice that the spirits submit to you, but rejoice that your names are written in Heaven." Then verse 21 follows with Jesus saying that he was "full of joy through the Holy Spirit" at this time and offered up prayers of praise to the Father. In praising the work of John the Baptist, he said that John was greater than any of the prophets who had come before him. Jesus made a habit of offering praise to others for their faith or good deeds. He was and is a rewarder.

Was unity important? Check!

Just before Jesus entered Jerusalem that final week, his plea for his disciples was to have one basic outcome to their faith and love: *unity through him alone.* God created man in order to have a relationship with him. That is clear from the accounts of Adam, Abraham, Moses, David, Elijah, and on throughout the Bible. He wants a loving relationship with his creation. He has provided everything necessary for that to happen, but he requires one thing in return, and that is simple faith. In Ephesians 2:8, Paul says for a second time in the same chapter that we are saved by his grace, but notes that it is through faith that we access that saving grace. It is a gift Jesus provided us by substituting his death for ours as payment for our sin. This is the extent to which God longs for a relationship with his created beings. Faith allows access to that grace, and loving grace is what allows for an eternal relationship with him that begins on Earth.

Earlier in their experience with Jesus, even the chosen twelve were subject to the pull of the flesh, and they were centered on their own interests. They wanted to know who would be the greatest in the new kingdom and who might sit at the right hand of God even at the end. But after the resurrection, the disciples did not worry anymore about who was first. Once they had committed to the mission with trust, loyalty, and love, and once they understood the meaning of the risen Savior, they became unified in their purpose of spreading the Gospel to the uttermost parts of Earth. Each disciple had a different role, but they all remained friends to the end, committed to their faith and their mission, victors in every way—a victory that has endured. Now the challenge is ours.

As a team builder today Jesus would have mercy and patience, but total tolerance for everything he sees in this world would be out of the question. God was extremely jealous of foreign gods in the Old Testament. He came to Earth in human form and showed mankind a better way of life through faith in him, so I do not envision his being willing to wink at the various idols we often put before him. He wants an exclusive relationship with his creation.

Meaningful relationships formed and valued? Check!

Luke 10:38–42 gives an example the kind of relationships Jesus formed. Jesus had come to have dinner with his friends Lazarus, Mary, and Martha. In her intent to serve Jesus and his disciples,

Martha had her hands full. She was doing all she could do to get everything in order, not only because the custom of the day was to provide great hospitality, but especially because of her great desire to serve her friend and mentor.

Ultimately, she became upset, as things piled up, and she fell behind. Tired of trying to do it all herself, she noted that her sister, Mary, was sitting at the feet of Jesus, drinking in all that he was saying. Mary was not lifting a finger to help her sister Martha serve the group. Maybe she had given Mary a few looks or "ahems" to no avail, so she went directly to Jesus and asked if he didn't care that "my sister" (not even calling her by name) had left her to do all the work (that is, serving). In answering Martha, Jesus made the point about the "main thing," "Martha, Martha, you are worried and troubled by many things, but *one thing* is needed. Mary (not "your sister") has chosen the *best part;* it will not be taken away from her."

This is not to diminish the need to serve, nor minimize its importance as part of Christian life. But the order is clearly made that relating to Jesus comes first, while serving, with its rewards, results from that relationship. He did not discount what Martha was doing, but the point that can be drawn from this narrative is that formalistic serving ought to be avoided. The relationship gives meaning to service. Scriptural Christian teaching requires that Jesus comes first in one's heart, and serving him comes second, as a response.

As has often been said, it is important to "keep the main thing the main thing." Having a relationship with the true God is the "main thing." Serving comes as a result of believing in Jesus, and regarding him as the "main thing." Service that springs from that relationship becomes "kingdom work," and such actions will have eternal rewards. But this is what one does subsequent to salvation;

it is not the way to attain eternal life, according to New Testament teaching. The price for salvation, the debt for sin, was paid once and for all on the cross on behalf of those who believe and follow (I John 2:2 and 4:10; Hebrews 9:26 and 10:10; Romans 3:25).

OTHER SCRIPTURAL REFERENCES
TO ERASE SELF-DOUBTS

Feel inadequate?

Obviously, the references to Jesus's life and leadership can be overwhelming when we consider our own weaknesses and shortcomings. For this reason, let's examine some other biblical examples that give encouragement.

Our first example is Moses. Here was a man who started in life with an immediate death sentence and was literally "up the creek without a paddle." But God had a plan for him that would not be revealed until much later. Moses grew up in the home of the Pharaoh, the most powerful man in that part of the world, only to become a fugitive in a far-off land after killing a man who was abusing a fellow Hebrew. After many years of his new life in that country, he encountered a burning bush that could talk better than he could.

Through that bush God told Moses that he needed a point man and he had a mission for him. Moses hesitated greatly when he heard it required him to return to his native Egypt. He feared going back, where he was a fugitive and a wanted man. He protested that he couldn't speak well enough. How would he be able to convince anyone to listen to him? So God gave him a helper as a spokesperson, his brother Aaron. God also gave Moses tools—a staff that became a serpent when he threw it down but changed back when he picked it up again—and he could change his hand to leprous and back to whole on command. Once Moses understood, accepted, and committed to his new mission, he had the confidence and courage to challenge the Pharaoh face-to-face in order to free his people. When we are willing to serve, God supplies the power and the tools—we can call them power tools.

Too young or too damaged?

Another biblical example of someone who answered the call to be a point person is that of David. While we generally think of him as a conquering warrior, he did not start out in life that way. He was the youngest son in his family and was not brought to the interview with the prophet Samuel when Samuel visited Jesse, David's father. Samuel was sent by God to select one of Jesse's sons to be Saul's successor as king of Israel. Young David was out in the fields doing the work of a humble commoner—a shepherd. Who would expect God to use a son from the line of David, Jesus the carpenter, to be the Good Shepherd and king of kings?

David was the baby of the house, the youngest of eight sons and, apparently, a sensitive lad who was gifted as a musician and poet. These are not the normal pastimes of a warrior-king prototype. Though he was strong in body and spirit, his brothers probably thought of him as a nerd or geek. He appeared to be the eighth man on an eight-man roster. To the big brothers he was definitely a sub, a role player at best. He was working his way up from the bottom by shepherding. But, of course, God thrives through man's weakness, and David was God's man.

Even after being chosen and anointed by Samuel to be the future king, young David went back out to tend his sheep. What? Think of that in modern terms. When young men not more than two or three years older than David was at the time receive a lucrative professional sports contract today, many cannot wait to do crazy things with their newfound wealth. When adults hit the lottery, many take a direction that ruins their lives. But "king" David went back out to check on the sheep. This is a picture of how Jesus, the great shepherd, would represent himself. He knew his sheep by name because he cared for them. People on point express humility by their actions. Someone had to tend those sheep. That was David's attitude.

Later, when asked by his father to take some food to his older brothers, who were fighting against the Philistines, the teenager gladly went as a servant for his father and brothers. Think of how many of our modern teenagers might respond to such a request. It could go something like, "Are you talking to me? Do I look like the pizza delivery boy? You are talking to the king here. We can find someone else to go."

Amazingly, when he arrived at the battlefield, his older brother met him with disdain and chided him for having the audacity to talk to the soldiers about the standoff that was taking place. But when a champion was called for, it wasn't the brother or even King Saul but young David who would accept the challenge to fight Goliath. He was the one willing to sacrifice himself for his loved ones to determine which nation would be declared the winner. He clearly understood what was needed.

1. He understood the mission: to save his people. He focused on God and the goal, not the Giant.

2. He was aware he represented a higher power whose authority was being challenged.

   He was willing to be God's ambassador and believed God would save him from harm because he knew God favored him.

3. He analyzed the situation and came up with a plan to win the battle.

4. He judged his strength and his opponent's weakness. He had the advantage of speed and the element of surprise in his trusty sling, which had saved him from animal attacks in the fields.

   He took five stones, not because he might miss but because Goliath was not the only giant on the Philistine team.

5. He ran to his task with enthusiasm and confidence even though Goliath made light of him with a Philistine version of "trash talk."

6. Unafraid, David announced he would cut off Goliath's head with the giant's own sword.

7. He executed his game plan to defeat Goliath with a single stone and gave the credit for his success to the Lord.

A further illustration of David's humility can be seen in his visits to Saul's palace where he played a harp to soothe the king's incapacitating headaches (1 Samuel 16:14–23). Apparently David had never brought it up to King David; he just did his job. Although David already knew he would be the next king, incredibly, Saul had to ask David who he was and who his father was after David killed the giant (1 Samuel 17:55–58). Although there were some glitches in David's life along the way, all too familiar to those of us living in human bodies, David would continue to stay with his mission to be God's man throughout his adult life. He is the one man specifically referred to as having a "heart for God" (1 Samuel 13:14).

The ongoing lesson is that God encourages us by often choosing humble, weak, or flawed people to do his work. He chose the shepherd David. He selected simple fishermen and uneducated Galileans. This should be a source of encouragement for us all.

Have too difficult a task to do or opponents to overcome?

Then consider Nehemiah, in the Book of Nehemiah. He led the reconstruction of Jerusalem after the Israelites' devastating years of captivity in Babylon. Due to their rejection of God in the years after David, both Israel and Judah were destroyed, and most of the surviving inhabitants were carried off as captives. Nehemiah was a Judean leader, who worked his way into a relationship with the Babylonian king, Artaxerxes, and whose mission was to restore his homeland. Nehemiah had great communication skills that enabled him to become close to the strongest king in that part of the world. He became his cupbearer, and he did it as a captive foreigner. The king agreed to let him leave his court but wanted him to return, such being the strength of their relationship. Nehemiah exhibited his humility when he explained the sources of his power were his heavenly king and his earthly king.

When Nehemiah arrived in Jerusalem, he witnessed its total devastation. All the buildings had been demolished, and the walls around the city had been destroyed. Moreover, local enemies sought to harm him. But he was committed to the vision given to him by

God, and he had the passion and enthusiasm that drew others to him and his mission. This enabled him to persuade others to dedicate themselves to the task. So with tools in one hand and weapons in the other, they proceeded to rebuild the city.

The second chapter of the book of Nehemiah gives a good account of his game plan and team-building skills. He began his speech to the people he depended on to get the work done by pointing to the destruction. Instead of scolding, however, he appealed to their pride and to their emotions. As he pointed out the obvious desolation, he asked rhetorically, "Do you want to live any longer in disgrace?" Humbly, yet authoritatively, he urged them to join him in the great task of rebuilding. He didn't shame them further, and he didn't say that he would rebuild the city or that he had work for them to do. Instead he spoke of the trouble both he and they were in and called on all to join him. He made it clear that he would join them in the task when he said, "Let us start rebuilding."

He convinced them that what they had considered impossible was, in fact, quite possible. He indicated authority and responsibility would be shared while never using the first-person singular. This was going to be a cooperative operation. As a point man, he recruited them to be on his team in perfect team-building style.

There is a great lesson here. Just because something is immensely difficult or has not been done for a long time (or ever) is no reason to think it cannot be done at all. It took more than three generations before someone was willing to act as a point man for the Jews in captivity. And as monumental as the operation was, Nehemiah risked his life to enact the vision God had given him. He applied the method alluded to in our wheels for team building—and it worked for him.

There are many great examples of leadership throughout the Hebrew scriptures. We learn much about persistence in the narrative of Noah, who took about a century to build an ark before it began to rain. Such patience in the face of extreme criticism and continual questioning was extraordinary. We struggle when we are criticized for ten minutes today—imagine a hundred years' worth of it.

Joshua showed the value of confidence through faith, combined with humble obedience to the God's game plan when he led the Hebrew nation into enemy territory armed with only horns and lanterns, as God had instructed. God has a plan for each one of us and has supplied the tools with which to accomplish this plan, once we commit to following him and seek to do his kingdom's work. In his book *Kingdom Man*, Tony Evans notes that "there are no unnecessary players on a football team and there are no less valuable positions in God's kingdom."[8] We may choose not to fulfill our roles, but the plan is there, as are the tools.

That doesn't mean it will be easy

In all these examples we can see the value of what we may refer to as a wilderness experience: those moments when people on point must go through pain, suffering, and disappointment before realizing their goals. While many of the judges and kings of Israel and Judah fell because of arrogance, fear, or lack of faith, the great ones succeeded through their struggles. Arguably, they advanced because of their struggles. They prevailed despite setbacks, just as most athletes, businessmen, and inventors do to be successful. Such struggles in our own wilderness experiences help to produce the humility and dependency needed to unleash God's spiritual power into our lives.

---

8 Evans, Tony. *Kingdom Man*. Carol Stream, IL: Tyndale, 2012, 97.

Know that no limitations have been placed on us

No one is ever disqualified because of age, position, or a sinful past. Abraham and Sarah were not too old to start a new nation of people. David, the teenager, was not too young. The tax collectors, Matthew and Zacchaeus, were not too sinful. And being a woman was not a deterrent, even being a prostitute, as proven by the contributions of many women, including Rahab, Esther, Mary Magdalene, and other women followers who stayed with Jesus all the way to the tomb. We never know if our task will be big or small, but we do know God has plans for us (Jeremiah 29:11) and once we are in him, he reveals the work he has prepared for us to do (Ephesians 2:9–10).

Whose will is it anyway? Perhaps you are someone who says, "I pray to know his will for my life, but I am never sure I am getting an answer or only hearing the echo of my own voice. I am just not sure what God wants me to do." If this what you've been thinking, you are probably already in his will or close to learning it. These are exactly the questions he wants us to ask. And the answer is that we are doing his will in our present and future circumstances as long as we are with Christ Jesus and seek to follow his will. His commands are the same now as they were 2,000 years ago. Simply stated, he wants us to honor him in what we do and love one another. He will bless our efforts when we offer our minds and souls and strength for his use. He blesses kings and paupers. He blesses those who rule nations and those who simply speak a word of truth, or do an act of kindness in his name (Matt. 22:37–39 and 1 Cor. 10:31). In turn, he expects us to use his blessings to bless others. My constant prayer is to be a blessing to others. I am hoping this book will be one.

STUDY

1. In what ways did Jesus show his desire for companionship?

2. What were some examples of Jesus's communication skills?

3. What is your reaction to the statement that people sometimes overemphasize service?

4. Explain how Jesus showed a range of human emotions, demonstrating his humanity.

5. Explain how the divine selection of David, the disciples, the tax collectors, and the woman at the well should be of comfort to us.

CHAPTER SIX

REAPING EXTRA BENEFITS BY BEING ON POINT

There will be thankfulness and joy

Many benefits will accrue as you strive to become more influential on your Life-Teams. Helping others brings benefits to the helper as well. In the previous chapters, we have mentioned at length the importance of love, humility, encouragement, persistence, trust, loyalty, and unity in successful team building. But these qualities also can build character noted by thanksgiving and joy. In 1 Thessalonians 5:16–18, Paul combines joy with thankfulness in the same complex sentence covering three verses: "Be joyful always; pray continually; give thanks in all circumstances, for this is God's will for you in Christ Jesus."

Please take note that, as a bonus in Paul's message to the Thessalonians, having a heart of joy and giving thanks is another indicator of being in God's will. As mentioned earlier, doing God's will is not as complex as we often make it out to be. Do you ever worry about your faith when you give thanks for the things you are doing? And can you experience real joy when you know you are in a sinful situation? There is a difference between excitement and joy. Sin often offers the former, but never the latter.

In Colossians 3:17, Paul also denotes the value of a heart of gratitude: "Whatever you do, whether in word or deed, do it all in the name of the Lord Jesus, giving thanks to God the Father through him." This is a clarion call for you to show your gratitude through every word you speak and deed you do. Note the urgency of the word "all" that is used in both the above quotations. Give thanks as you do everything—not sometimes, or frequently, or always in certain situations, or to a select group of people.

Joy and Thanksgiving come with the Wheels

In the letter to the Philippians, Paul not only expresses the hope of attaining complete joy, but gives total credence to many of the qualities in our wheels system that equip a person to be on point. The italicized words in Philippians 2:1–3 confirm points we have emphasized in the foregoing chapters:

"Therefore, if there is any *encouragement* in Christ, if there is any consolation of *love*, if there is any *fellowship* (i.e., relationship) of the Spirit, if any *affection* and compassion, make my *joy* complete by being of the *same mind*, maintaining the same *love, united* in spirit, *intent* on *one purpose*. Do nothing from selfishness or empty conceit, but with *humility* of mind *regard one another* as more important than yourselves."

The Scripture here bears repeating often on one's journey through life. It covers the essence of the wheels we have constructed for building up our Life-Teams in a scriptural context from mission to unity and relationships. Joy and thanksgiving are natural by-products of successful team building and are continuing evidence of good relationships on the Life-Team.

Why don't we hear more about joy?

It is amazing how often the concept of joy appears in the Bible—more than two hundred times. This will come as a surprise to those who have alluded to the Puritan's dour representation of faith, which still exists among rules-oriented parishioners in some churches today. We are admonished to seek and find joy in the various roles we play in life, but human nature seems intent on finding circumstances and events to complain about or criticize. I have a personal struggle in this area. Let me give you an example of a lesson I learned, one that I am still trying to apply to my life. In the 2004 Olympics, as the first foreigner to be named coach of the national basketball team of China, I felt sorry for myself because of the problems I was encountering. We had inadequate housing and we lacked equipment other teams possessed, such as game film of the opposing teams, and editing equipment, among a host of other problems. We faced a nearly impossible task, it seemed.

Before continuing, I want to discuss one of my favorite stories from the Old Testament, because it is relevant to my Olympic experience. The narrative is that of Gideon from the seventh chapter of Judges. Israel continually fought against one group of "-ites" or another when they invaded the Promised Land. Gideon was called upon to lead Israel against one of these forces, the Midianites. Their massive army seemed innumerable and insurmountable. Gideon initially rounded up an army of 32,000 men, but God systematically cut his squad down to 300 to go against what seemed like a "swarm of locusts" encamped on a nearby mountain. Not only did God pare down the troops, he reduced their armaments supply to two weapons of "mass destruction:" trumpets and torches.

But Gideon, the point man of the moment, was armed with faith, which is why he was chosen to lead in the first place. He knew the mission and became committed to the game plan. At the proper moment during the night, he launched a surprise attack with trumpets blaring and torches glaring. The Midianites figured if the enemy had that many trumpeters, they would have no chance against the massive contingent of warriors that must be following. Surprised and confused, they began to question the leadership, the scouts, and the battle plan. They scattered and fought against one another. Gideon's "army" completely routed them. Later, when questioned about his great victory, Gideon answered that God alone had delivered the enemy into Israel's hands, which was true, of course. But Gideon was thankful and joyful.

What does that story have to do with my experience at the Athens Olympics of 2004, you may be wondering? There was a time I felt like Gideon. Let me give you seven reasons for that:

1. I took the job to coach with the idea I would have four assistants, and I ended up with two: a Chinese coach, who spoke no English, and an English-speaking Lithuanian coach. The latter was a good coach, but he missed the last five weeks of practice and games prior to the Olympics due to a back injury, and he was not with us at the beginning of the Olympic Games.

2. Yao Ming, the best player by far, came to camp a month after I had started with the team that would be built around him. He was out of shape and was suffering foot problems that caused him to miss some practice games and to play with damaged feet in the ones he did play. During the Olympic Games, his feet were so bad that his socks

would be red from bleeding after each game. Despite all that, I have to say he was a true warrior and a wonderful person to coach and know. They operated on his feet after the games, but he has continued to have foot problems since then. This was the reason he had to retire early from the NBA.

3. My team was placed in the toughest bracket. The weakest opposing team had finished fourth in the world championships two years earlier and all their players in those championships returned for the Olympic Games. Twelve NBA players finished sixth in that same tournament in Indianapolis.

4. I was unable to get any game film of the opponents until two days before the games began. Other teams had films for weeks.

5. We had no video equipment and, to compound the problem, the Chinese officials had not signed up to have all the games cabled into our room as the other teams had.

6. I had to catch a cab and venture into Athens to buy three VCRs and two monitors. I fortunately managed to borrow film from coaching friends from Australia, Lithuania, and Greece—teams in the opposing bracket. I became my team's coach/video coordinator guy.

7. I was put in a 900-square-foot apartment with six other people for seventeen days, and we started out with no hot water for three days. There were other things too, but seven is a good number for lists.

As far as the difficult bracket was concerned, initially I was glad that we had to play Serbia on the last day of the medal-qualifying round. I figured maybe we could beat New Zealand and Italy, until the latter beat the US team ten days earlier in a pre-Olympics tournament. The Italian team proved to be so strong it would go on to win the silver medal in this Olympics, a step ahead of the United States. I believed we would have very little chance against Spain, which finished with the best record at 7–1 but lost at the wrong time to win a medal, and Argentina, which won the championship gold. I assumed we would have even less of a chance against Serbia, the defending world champions. They had beaten us easily by twenty points just ten days earlier in Belgrade, winning a tournament that also included Argentina, Lithuania, and Australia. I anticipated the Serbian team would know where it stood by the time we played it, since it would be the last game for us both in the preliminary round. I thought that if the game were not important to them, as far as qualifying for the medal round was concerned, maybe they would not take us too seriously.

After our first game, things looked pretty bad. Spain hammered us by twenty-five points, and New Zealand looked really good when they lost by only three points to the impressive Italian team. But my capable Lithuanian assistant, Jonas Kaslauskas, arrived after the game with Spain, and that lifted me a little. We played a very good game, beating New Zealand on the second day, and that provided a ray of hope. Had we lost that one, we would've basically been out of it after only two games because we would have to win two of the next four games against extremely tough competition. In our third game, two days later, Argentina ran away from us by twenty points, and Italy did the same on the following day. In the meantime, Serbia had been upset in close games by Spain, Italy, and Argentina, which went right down to the wire. Lo and behold, they were in the same situation as we were. Each team had beaten New Zealand but had to win this last game or be eliminated from competing in the medal round.

We now had a day of preparation before going up against Serbia in a must-win situation. This was a really bad scenario for us, and the Chinese delegation didn't appear to be happy with the coach. I was glad I had not learned Chinese at that point, but I understood international body language. The Chinese federation wanted its young team to get into the medal round to prepare it for the competition of the 2008 Beijing Olympics.

All this time I was reading the Bible every day, as is my custom. One of the passages I depended on was Ephesians 2:4–10, one I repeat often as life verses. I focused specifically on verse 10. That verse indicates that God has works for me to do, which he has prepared in advance. I accepted the Olympics job in the belief that my coaching in the NBA and around the world had uniquely prepared me for it. I had coached in the NBA for thirty years and had successfully represented three other countries in world competitions, giving me incredible international experience. In addition, I reminded myself of the familiar Romans 8:28 verse, in which Paul says that God makes things work for those who love him and are called according to his purpose. I saw my Olympics endeavor as God-given. I was led to 2 Thessalonians 1:11–12, which states that Paul prayed for people to be "found worthy of their calling." If we did not win this game, none of these thoughts would be validated in a way I had expected, because the loser would be out.

A key moment came as I read my Bible. After feeling sorry for myself, I decided to accept my situation, although I was disappointed, really down. But I did my video edits and read my verses. This time I turned to 2 Peter 1:3–9: "*His divine power has given us everything we need* for life and godliness through our knowledge of him, who called us by his own glory and goodness … For this very reason, make every effort to *add to your faith* goodness; and to goodness, knowledge; and to knowledge, self-control; and to self-control perseverance; and to perseverance, godliness; and to godliness, brotherly kindness; and to brotherly kindness, love. If you possess these qualities in *increasing measure*, they will keep *you from being ineffective* and unproductive in your knowledge of our Lord Jesus Christ." Notice the words I have italicized to understand the message I received.

What these verses told me was: God would provide the power, but I had to supply the attitude. These verses asked me to make every effort to *increase* in the basic areas of spirituality noted in Galatians 5:22. They didn't assume that I already *owned* all these qualities in abundance. I was reminded that our walk through life is a *progression*, even though *perfection* is out of reach, except through grace. I became more aware that I didn't have to have all these items down pat yet, or that I ever could for that matter. I needed to work through the power of the Spirit to *increase* and develop my attitudes. Life is about working to get better just as I tell my basketball players concerning their abilities on the court. But I was still somewhat down.

Then an even bigger moment occurred, as I happened to glance over to see a scripture on the page opposite the Thessalonians verse that I was reading. This was providential. There on that page was 1 Thessalonians 5:16, which told me to "be joyful always."

Now wait a minute—no staff, no game film, no help, and Yao wasn't coming up big. World Champion Serbia was up next, and I was supposed to be joyful? I was expected to be peaceful and gentle and kind and self-controlled?

Back to Gideon and the current battle

That is when I thought about Gideon, and it reaffirmed that I was surely called to do this work. That had to be the case. Maybe I was to be put in the worst possible position so I would know his power and not mine was what I should depend on. I decided that God would not have sent me over there to fail. Upon that assumption, I put two sticky notes on my wall as reminders—"Gideon" and "PTL"—and determined to go into the game with the idea that I was going to coach it the best way I could, with the right spirit. I would see what happened. I was going to be joyful for the opportunity I had been given, good calls or bad calls, made shots or missed shots. I reflected on the many opportunities given me, a small-town boy, in my long professional career. To think I was the first foreigner to be coach of this huge nation's team, and I got to experience one of life's unique thrills: parading at the opening night of the Olympics in Athens where it had all started so long ago. What a thrill! And many more thankful thoughts flooded my mind, about my family, my health, and numerous other blessings. When I did this, a peace came over me that I had never felt before a big game. It was wonderful. Sounds crazy maybe, but it's true.

We started the game off aggressively and were able to get the ball inside to Yao more easily than expected. At halftime we were tied, and I was relieved, thinking that we were at least making a decent showing. It still had not occurred to me that we might actually win the game, but Serbia had decided in their game plan that, unlike every other opponent we had faced, they did not have to double-team Yao. Everyone else trapped Yao on each catch, forcing our other players to beat them, but Serbia seemed to think they were above that tactic. As the second half wore on, we kept hanging around, staying close until, with about three minutes remaining in the game, we tied the score. When we went ahead by a point, it was almost like Gideon's battle in which the Midianites became so confused they started going after one another. As the seconds ticked off, the Serbians fought among themselves. Their ever-emotional head coach, the one whom the Serbs had advertised as the best coach in the world, began to unravel as well.

The last two minutes went back and forth, up one or two points and down one or two. With thirty seconds to play we went up by two points, and we got a key defensive stop. To stop the clock, they fouled one of my players, a sub, but he made two free throws to put us up by four. They countered with two points of their own, but then had to foul the same player again with four seconds to go— and he made both free throws for another four point lead. Serbia thought they were fouling a player not good enough to be a starter. Guess what? That sub was in the game at the end because he was my best foul shooter. He was playing his role and being our person on point. They made a half-court three-pointer at the buzzer, but it didn't matter. It was "game over" for what is still one of my most memorable wins in more than fifty years of coaching. Yao had scored over half of our points on bloody feet. In the aftermath, the Serbian head coach resigned his position, abandoning his troops. Amazing!

In the joyous locker room, filled with nearly incredulous players and team reps, I knew I had to say something. I had not said much to the players in terms of religion, since my only venture into it had been cut off really fast by one of our players. He had turned the subject to basketball in a hurry. But after that game I called for silence and said, "I want everyone to know that in my religion I am required by faith to give credit and thanks to God for this great moment and I do that now." There was no reaction of any kind, and after a brief silence, the jubilation continued. Yes, I was joyful. And thankful.

I don't know what will come of all of that experience. I know that there are a lot of Chinese people who are searching for truth. China has historically been a nation of believers, a religious people. But Communism voided that and the Chinese made Communism the source of their faith. Now that they have found strict Communism cannot deliver all that was promised, a vacuum exists in China in terms of faith. A close friend of Yao explained this to me one day at lunch. There are millions of Christians in China and there are believers of other faiths as well, but most are not out in the open about their religious beliefs. While a state Christian church is allowed, it is not what it seems to be. The government has total control over it, and many of the basic tenets of the religion cannot be taught in the churches or at the universities.

I am glad for the time spent with my Chinese players and for the relationships we established, which have continued to this day. I have returned to China a few times to give clinics, along with coach John Calipari. On one of these occasions, in 2009, my Chinese hosts organized had a big night with a presentation at a dinner to mark my fiftieth year in coaching. My task for the 2004 Olympics was to take a young group of players and get them ready to make a good showing in the 2008 Olympics in Beijing. And they were able to do that. Jonas Kaslauskas, the Lithuanian who was my assistant coach in 2004, stayed on for four years to work with the team. They finished in eighth position, the same position in which we finished in Athens, but they were a much more mature team and more competitive in their losses than we had been in Athens. Jonas did a great job, and the entire four-year endeavor is regarded as a huge success in China. The team still regards the win against Serbia to be its best-ever victory.

We have a joy component, apparently

From the start of Jesus's life, the angel brought "good news of great joy, which will be for all the people" (Luke 2:10). Jesus later said, "These things I have spoken to you so that my joy may be in you and your joy may be made full," and in another passage, "Ask and you will receive, so that your joy may be made full" (John 15:11 and 16:24). Read it again and think about it. We have arms, legs, a head, and so on, and Jesus is saying we also have a "joy." But do we recognize it? I had never seen it as perhaps a "muscle" that I am not working out adequately. If it is a muscle, I have let it go the way of my abs. We have already cited Paul's admonition in Philippians to be joyful. I am embarrassed that I do not stop and feel the emotion of joy more often. We have a built-in joy factor and Jesus recognized that it was not always full. So if it is more like a gas tank, why do we go around with our "joy tanks" on half-full or even empty? We need to check our gauges more often, obviously.

Fruit is not always in season?

When Paul speaks of the fruit of the Spirit in Gal. 5:22, his first two points are about love and joy. It is really hard to love others all the time, and it is humanly impossible to express joy in every situation. Still, there is a season for all these things. Fruit is not always in season, as we well know. Sometimes it is hard to be loving, joyful, gentle, kind, patient, and so forth. Joy doesn't readily come to mind when tragedy strikes, or when we are in severe pain. But overall, our lives can be defined by joyfulness. We often lose our hold on self-control, but we must keep working to lengthen our productive season. No one bears these fruits all the time. In reality Jesus was not always joyful. He had moments of frustration with the Pharisees. But he was joyful when joy was called for, and he wants us to be joyful over the general course of our lives, counting even our sufferings and wilderness experiences as joy when we have time to reflect on them. Fortunately, God sees us and our fruit through the eyes of his amazing grace, as opposed to judging us on a purely factual basis. He regards us as not yet grown but growing. He asks us to increase in these areas.

Thankfulness and joy are states of being

It has often been said that we should live with an "attitude of gratitude." I believe that thankfulness is not as much an attitude as it is a state of being. There is probably only a fine line of difference, but attitudes can be manufactured and falsely presented, whereas a state of being is genuine by definition—that is, you are either in it or you are not. The importance of thankfulness has already been noted in the scripture from 1 Thessalonians that connects joy and gratitude. The thankful state of being is by nature one of peace, joy, and humility. The angry person is not in a thankful state. The arrogant person does not feel the need to thank anyone. He believes he has done it all himself and he deserves every good thing that comes his way. The assumption of entitlement blocks out gratitude. So does the audacity of presumed superior knowledge. These were the attitudes of Jesus's opponents in his time on Earth, and they prevented his opponents' acceptance of him, which led to his crucifixion. These are the same sentiments that prevent secularists in our current society from accepting him. Today, as in all previous times, God seeks minds that thirst for knowledge.

He works best through the heart that is open, humble, and thankful. A thankful heart will have joy. There is little else that needs to be said of the importance God places on a thankful heart. It is his will that we live our lives in thanks. And that should close the case on the importance of thankfulness.

Different responses to blessings — one thankful, one not so much

Two narratives in the New Testament describe different responses made by men who contemplated how they would deal with their success. The first is about a nameless, wealthy farmer, described in Luke 12:16–20: "The ground of a certain rich man yielded an abundant harvest. He thought to himself, 'What shall I do? I have no place to store my crops.' Then he said, 'This is what I will do. I will tear down my barns and build bigger ones, and there I will store my surplus grain. And I'll say to myself, 'You have plenty of grain laid up for many years. Take life easy; eat, drink and be merry."

The second story is that of Zacchaeus, the tax collector, found in Luke 19:1–10. "Jesus entered Jericho and was passing through. A man was there by the name of Zacchaeus; he was a chief tax collector and was wealthy. He wanted to see who Jesus was but, being a short man, he could not see because of the crowd. So he ran ahead and climbed a sycamore–fig tree to see him, since Jesus was coming that way. When Jesus reached the spot, he looked up and said to him, 'Zacchaeus, come down immediately, I must stay at your house today.' So he came down at once and welcomed him gladly. All the people saw this and began to mutter, 'He has gone to be the guest of a sinner.' But Zacchaeus stood up and said to the Lord, 'Look, Lord! Here and now I give half of my possessions to the poor, and if I have cheated anybody out of anything, I will pay back four times the amount.' Jesus said to him, 'Today salvation has come to this house, because this man, too, is a son of Abraham. For the Son of Man came to seek and to save what was lost.'"

In the reading of the two stories above we see a capsule version of the lives of two men who achieved worldly success but were consumed by the pursuit of material things. The farmer had done well with his fields and was feeling pretty good about himself. He had in mind early retirement from all the work he had put in, and there is nothing wrong with that in and of itself. He had two problems, however. The first was that he thought he had done it all by himself, and the second was what he planned to do, or better yet not to do, with his wealth. Jesus makes it perfectly clear that "the ground of a certain man produced the good crop," not the farmer. So the farmer's initial problem was arrogance. And that prevented him from being thankful for his blessings. His second issue was selfishness. He planned to quit the work, travel around the world, play golf, and fill that in with some eating, drinking, and generally having a good time with his wealth. He had no intention of helping others with his blessings. Arrogance and selfishness are a deadly combination. God said to him, "You fool! This very night your life will be demanded from you. Then who will get what you have prepared for yourself?'"

The second story is about a little guy whom we will call Zach for short, because he was. Little Zach was an outcast in his society, working for the government in the IRS department, headquartered in Rome. The way it worked was that he would charge taxes on behalf of the Roman authorities, and he had a quota he had to come up with to keep his job and his head. What he could charge above that amount was his to keep. With the backing of the Roman military, most tax collectors overcharged as much as they could and became quite wealthy. It was a pretty good gig—no inventory and a nice cash flow.

Zach, apparently, was not totally like most other taxmen. There was a spark in him that God was able to use, just as he had with that other taxman, Matthew. That spark stirred Zach to climb up a tree so he could see Jesus. Zach had a mission that day. The scripture reads clearly, "He wanted to see Jesus." So, once Zach got a glimpse of him, he shouted out, "Hey Jesus, you and your boys look a little hungry. How about coming over to my place for din-din tonight? I have the best house around these parts, got my own chef—good kosher stuff."

No, actually Jesus looked up and called him by name and announced, "I am inviting myself and my guys here to your house for dinner tonight, so get down out of that tree before you fall and break your neck."

Now, it is not politically correct in our society to invite ourselves to dinner, but in that day it was a compliment of high honor for an important person to request the hospitality of another. And Jesus was honoring this man, whom everyone in town saw as a low-life sinner. But Zach was open; he was curious. He wanted to see Jesus. Openness is all Jesus asks, because he wants to sit with us. Once in the presence of Jesus, Zach was changed forever. He looked at his wealth and instead of wanting to go out and charge more so he could entertain Jesus and any other dignitary who passed through in the future, he decided to share it with those who were less fortunate. He gave half to the poor, and he was going to repay in quadruple those he had overcharged. This was a voluntary act of contrition and commitment. This was not government welfare. This was giving from the heart by a changed and thankful man.

Look at the epilogues to each of those accounts of two wealthy men. We don't even know the name of the farmer to whom Jesus said, "You fool! This very night your life will be required of you. You were rich to yourself, but you did not seek to honor God the Father." Whereas Jesus proclaimed to Zach, "Today, salvation has come to this house."

Let's relate that to Romans 12:2: "Do not conform any longer to the pattern of this world, but be transformed by the renewing of your mind, and then you will be able to test and approve what God's will is." It is natural to want to "build bigger barns," to conform to the society, to do what most people do. We need to transform our way of thinking like Zach did. We must change our position in Jesus. Once we unite with Jesus, we see through a different mindset and form our opinions anew. The Spirit within us transforms our thinking, and we can "test and approve what God's will is."

And we know from Scripture that his will involves loving God and one another and that he wants us to be joyful and thankful. How do we find joy and show thanks? By building bigger barns? No. By giving and serving others like Zach, the taxman. He was joyful and thankful. He became a point man.

STUDY

1. Which of the descriptions of fruit of the Spirit found in Galatians 5:22 is most difficult for you?

2. Comment on what 2 Peter 1:8 can mean for us in our walk.

3. In the narrative of the Foolish Farmer, what do you make of the number of times "I," "me" or "mine" is used in the story? Count them.

4. Read Romans 12:6–13 and relate how Paul's capsule version of serving leadership and team building compares with the presentation in this book. Pretty amazing.

5. Make two columns and list all that you can be joyful for under one heading and then all you are thankful for under the other. What is your conclusion?

CHAPTER SEVEN

WHAT HAPPENS THAT GETS IN OUR WAY?

I n becoming more effective as a person on point, there are so many factors that can go wrong along the way that may interfere with our ability to improve our life-teams in our businesses, our institutions or our families. Each of these entities has its own unique features and structure, but we can benefit from identifying a few potential pitfalls and, perhaps, fit them into our own situation. Such is the advantage of the sports idiom. It reflects real life in many instances. This is why I like to start with sports analogies and then draw down what are general truths for other endeavors. So let's consider a few of the various factors that may need to be addressed and rectified when seeking to improve a situation affecting our personal or corporate Life-Teams.

You may need to re-evaluate your strategy

If you feel stagnant or held back from achieving more in life, one reason could be your hesitancy to make a change of some kind. Making changes is difficult for us humans. In 1981, I was head coach of the Houston Rockets. We were going along through the season, trying to play in the same style as the rest of the league and the same one I generally preferred to teach. The pro game was very fast-paced in those days, but we were getting nowhere playing that way. I had always had great success with an aggressive offensive attack, going back to my public-school and college coaching days. One of my Earlham College teams averaged 101.6 points per game prior to the insertion of the three-point shot, for example. Most players like to play that way, making the job of coaching easier, and fans tend to enjoy that style. We were averaging 110 points per game well after the middle of the season, but we didn't have the depth or the overall firepower to outscore a lot of teams. To gain some perspective, you should consider that between 1977 and 1987 an NBA team only failed to average more than 100 points per game for the season five times, quite unlike the NBA of the twenty-first century. The league leader in 1981, Denver, scored an incredible 121.8 per outing. But that was then. Since 1995 over half of all NBA teams have averaged less than 100 points per game for the season, and most of them are distraught when they allow an opponent to score more than 100 points.

The Rockets were scoring but muddling along, several games under .500, going into the last third of the season, when I decided we had to change our game paradigm. However, it took me a while to pull the trigger, and we kept going downhill. Finally, we adjusted our attack by playing a slower power game, utilizing our two centers in the starting lineup—all-star and future Hall of Famer Moses Malone and Billy "The Whopper" Paultz.

I really didn't prefer the slower-paced game, but I liked losing a lot less. I was on my second one-year contract with the Rockets. We had successfully changed gears with my last college team for one season because of a difference in our talent compared to those high-scoring years. Using the same concepts, we reduced the number of possessions in our game and focused on rebounding and better execution on the offensive end, combined with fewer turnovers and fouls. At first the Houston media mocked our strategy as "uglyball," but once we started to win, we became more attractive, and they called our team the Water Buffaloes. We played a slow game, but we became more effective.

We began to score below the 100-point mark, but we allowed even less than we were scoring—always a good thing. Then one day before our eighty-second game, Golden State lost, and that loss ensured us the twelfth and final spot in the play-offs. At that time fewer teams made the play-offs than today. At season's end we had won a total of only forty out of eighty-two games, but it was enough to get us a ticket to play the defending champion, Los Angeles Lakers, in the first round. These were the same Lakers who would win four more titles in the decade. Doesn't sound like much of a reward for such a great comeback, but even as a sub .500 team, we were able to upset them by beating them twice on their court. Fortunately for us, Moses Malone seemed to be able to manufacture some of his best games against Lakers center Kareem Abdul-Jabbar. He liked competing against the best.

Next came the San Antonio Spurs, an outstanding team, featuring Hall of Famer George Gervin and the Bruise Brothers, who had won our division by a wide margin. We beat them in seven games by winning an unlikely three games on their home court. In game seven of that great series, Hall of Famer Calvin Murphy, who had been our sixth man all year, was inserted into the starting lineup in order to help us to get off to a good start if possible. We wanted to avoid a slow start on San Antonio's court due to their loud and fanatical crowd. Equally as important was the fact that Malone had been ill the morning of the game and could not practice, so I was not sure how strong he would be that night.

The diminutive Murphy, one of only two players under six feet tall to play more than 1,000 NBA games, responded with forty-two points. Murph and Billy Paultz, who was big enough to set a double pick by himself, were able to pick and roll the Spurs into oblivion. Malone scored his normal twenty-eight points and grabbed a ton of rebounds, despite feeling subpar. Overall, the team played very well to give us a 105–100 win. Those three road wins gave us five wins away from home, and the team would ultimately set a record for road victories in a play-off series with eight. That record still ranks second all-time, having been broken by a later Rockets team on their way to a championship with nine road wins. That team won the 1995 title under coach Rudy Tomjanovich, who had been a player on this same record-setting team fourteen years earlier.

The Water Buffaloes played extremely well in winning the third round to gain the Western Conference Championship four games to one against the Kings. That win totally excited the entire city of Houston, giving the Bayou City its first big-league team ever to play for a national championship. To win, however, we had to beat the Boston Celtics, the team that had beaten us the year before in the second round of the play-offs in a sweep, when our franchise was still playing in the Eastern Conference. (League expansion put us in the Western Conference for the 1980–1981 season and subsequent ones.) Boston had vastly improved its team over the one we had lost to a year earlier by adding future Hall of Fame players Kevin McHale and Robert Parrish to go along with holdovers Larry Bird and another future Hall member, Tiny Archibald. This gave them four players who are now in the Hall of Fame (along with our Malone and Murphy). Boston also had a player named "Cornbread" Maxwell who remained from the 1980 team. Who would have thought that a guy named "Cornbread" would actually win the MVP trophy in a series that had six Hall of Fame players? But Maxwell was on a near par with those great players himself, and certainly was in that series.

The opener was played in Boston, of course, because the Celtics had won sixty-two games, a mere 55 percent more victories than the Rockets had managed, even with our late-season push. It appeared to be a classic mismatch. However, in the first game, victory was within reach, as we led most of the way. It took some late-game heroics by none other than Bird to beat us. He made the "best play I have ever seen," according to the great all-time coach, Red Auerbach, president of the Celtics at that time. The final score was 98–95. It was disappointing because we had won the first game in each of the three previous rounds and had come so close in this one. Still, the Rockets came back to win game two in another nail-biter in the Boston Garden, 92–90, thus capturing home-court advantage for the moment.

Boston bounced back big-time in game three at Houston with a raw display of power on both ends of the court on a Saturday, 94–71. Incredibly, by twenty-first-century standards, in which there may be as many as five days between some play-off games, game four was played on Sunday, the next afternoon. It was the most-watched game of the season on television. Of course, TV coverage was not as widespread then as it would become just a few years later. Still, millions were geared to see Bird and Company in action against the Cinderella Rockets. The Rockets played it slow and close to the vest the entire afternoon, using only six players in this back-to-back game, though that was not part of any pregame plan. It just worked out that way. But six players were enough as the underdog Red and White out-finessed the Big Green, 91–86. The series was knotted 2–2, and we headed back to Boston.

Boston broke game five open early and got an easy win, 109–80. But the Rockets were not done fighting. In game six back in Houston they took the Celtics down to the wire in what was a close game until the final minutes, when the Rockets had to foul to stop the clock. The final score was a misleading 101–90. There was no champion-ship ring for the Rockets, but the team had accomplished amazing things, setting multiple records in the process. They set all-time records for most offensive rebounds, fewest turnovers, plus the record for road wins and other more minor marks. No team since then has been seeded last and beaten the defending champions, nor has any post-1981 team with a sub .500 record made its way to the finals.

But we would never have been able to accomplish any of that had we not been willing to *evaluate* our position, *examine* what we were doing and *embark* on a new plan. It required the commitment of the entire team and coaching "staff." Staff is in quotes because there were only the two of us, my assistant Carroll Dawson and myself. But we had a great bunch of tough-minded guys, such as the two centers already mentioned, and Murphy, as well as Mike Dunleavy, Rudy Tomjanovich, Tommy Henderson, Robert Reid, Bill Willoughby, Major Jones, Allen Leavell, Calvin Garrett, and John Stroud. It was the same team that was losing, but I had the wrong system for that particular team makeup. Later Rockets teams would gain more acclaim for playing two centers in the lineup, Hakeem Olajuwon and Ralph Sampson, who were called the Twin Towers. But the big Water Buffaloes had paved the way for them.

To make this major turnaround, we didn't have to trade or fire anyone. We went with the players we had. We simply adjusted our strategy. Many other businesses and relationships have been saved without severe repercussions just by communicating and analyzing potential strategic changes of focus, attitudes, or demographic targets. You don't always have to blow up the entire deal to facilitate a favorable outcome. Overreaction should be a last resort, but no one should succumb to the comfort of inaction too readily either.

Your problem could be due to a power outage

Another cause for disappointment can be a breakdown in the power structure. It all starts at the top. In the NBA there is often a conflicting issue between the business side and the basketball side of the franchise. This translates into all kinds of other situations, including those in families, businesses, churches, and politics. Not everyone involved has the same agenda or is on the same page. It may be that the legal department within the corporation is having concerns about the CEO's direction that are real or imagined. It could be the board and the CEO are in a wrestling contest, the church board and the pastor could be at odds, or it might be the administration struggling against the faculty. The people in authority might be inhibiting one another's effectiveness and not be aware of it, or not be willing to admit it. All kinds of communication or relational problems may have to be examined, evaluated, and settled in order for progress to continue. Quite often, better communication can prevent real chaos, whether in a business, a church, an educational institution, or a home. Someone has to assume the point in order to get the program going in the right direction. That requires the skills we have noted in our discussions. A knowledge of the four wheels can be an important factor in salvaging a bad situation.

Maybe better sharing of authority could be a solution

The Dallas Cowboys fans have groaned and moaned for several years that the big problem with "America's Team" has been that their passionate owner, Jerry Jones, interferes too much. He has been the official GM, or de facto GM, and has gone through a merry-go-round of coaches, and roller-coaster seasons, in what has been described as a circus operation by critics. He has desperately put his heart, soul, and checkbook into the team but has won no Super Bowls since the mid-1990s. Meanwhile, in the NBA, the teams that have tended to do the best over the same period of time in terms of championships have been the Heat, Lakers, Spurs, Celtics, Pistons, and Bulls. It may or may not be coincidental, but the ownership of each of those franchises tends to be low-key and less involved. Either the coach or GM is the authority in those franchises, though they have normally worked in close harmony with the owner. But there is always next year for Cowboy fans.

You can do it right but still make the tough calls

Mark Cuban of the Mavericks has been somewhat of an exception. He has been the most hands-on owner of the successful NBA teams. The Mavs have won more regular-season games than any other team in the league during Cuban's tenure except for the Spurs. He finally grabbed the championship in 2011 in a classic victory in which team play outdistanced individual talent. In general he has been in harmony with the GM and the coach (at least until he wasn't) and particularly so with the virtual team leader, Dirk Nowitzki. But a huge key to Cuban's success may well be that he and GM Donnie Nelson have been particularly adamant about doing team-building exercises through providing an excellent environment, featuring good facilities, team dinners, and team events. He has provided the funds and encouraged the head coach to do team-promoting activities. He has a great passion for the mission, along with demonstrating over-the-top encouragement and excitement. He has shown a great personal concern for his players and has encouraged his coaches and the organization to do the same. He is consistently ready and willing to reward the players for achievement, as well as to trade them when he can upgrade the overall team. Players love playing for the Mavs, largely for these reasons, I believe. Cuban is a conscientious team builder, yet he has avoided the fatal flaw of becoming so emotionally attached to a player that he resists making the tough decisions when it is time to make a major move.

Super Bowl XLVI offers another example

Isn't it amazing what we can learn from champion teams? Here we go again. Robert Kraft is the owner of the New England Patriots, a team that has already won three Super Bowls in the twenty-first century. In an interview with David Moore of *The Dallas Morning News*, Kraft offered several nuggets of wisdom that attest to his team-building acumen. Kraft said, "You get good people with you, you set the tone, and you *encourage them* to be bold and take risks … that are in the best interests of the team."[9]

---

9 Moore, David. "Why Pats sizzle, 'Boys fizzle? NE's Kraft eliminates meddle man". *Dallas Morning News*, Feb. 7, 2012.

Kraft *trusts* his people to make good decisions and has placed faith and *power in the hands* of his coach, Bill Belichick. Kraft told Moore, "In the end, in the NFL, what happens often is division from within. Our job is always to get everyone on the same page and do the best we can." Further, Kraft proclaimed his overall purpose: "What I am trying to do with this team is *build relationships and let people know we care about them.*" No, I am not putting words in this man's mouth—just emphasizing them with the italics.

Are the people in the right position?

Babe Ruth would never have become the famous home-run hitter he became had he continued to be a pitcher, even though he was a very good one. Along that line it is significant to note an oft-told story of one of the great offensive football players of all time, Bo Jackson. He was just a good college defensive back until he was forced to move over to the offensive side of the ball due to injuries to Auburn's running backs. Only then did the coach see Jackson's Hall of Fame abilities that would propel him to become one of the greatest runners ever to play the game.

On the other hand, advancing a person to a different role may not be the best thing to do, even as a reward for a job well done. Sometimes the answer is to reward them in other ways and keep them in the area in which they are already succeeding. Keep in mind the famous Peter principle of promoting a person to the level of his incompetence. Along that line, good bench players don't always make good starters. Good sales people don't always make good managers. At the same time, it is important to show respect for the personal ambitions of colleagues and allow them some space to move up and either succeed or fail, yet be sensitive enough to reserve a parachute for valuable team members, even if they don't know they have it. If they are effective people, it is better to keep them on the team in some capacity, so long as they are content to remain in their best role.

Maybe the problem lies within ourselves

Obviously, our human condition works to hold us back. We are reticent to be humble, to serve, to encourage, to share authority, or to allow ourselves to be thankful and joyful. The best way to conquer it is to start working at it—that is to say, "Just do it." Commit to working at being encouraging every day, or find ways to share your power, or to be thankful. Look for ways to serve others in a spirit of humility. Try to sense joy by counting blessings. You can try this one item at a time until it gradually becomes a habit and part of a lifelong process of growing. Be patient, because growth comes in plateaus. The process may work better if one finds a partner—an accountability partner—to share in it, but that is not absolutely necessary.

Don't just sit there; take a risk!

Another thing that prevents some people from becoming all they could be is inaction. We accept too easily our status quo, even when it is not actually satisfying. We often tend to be unwilling to take a bit of a risk, to venture out of our comfort zone. We simply apply the excuse that "it is what it is" and resign ourselves to mediocrity or less. Psychologists say change is at the top of the list of the things that create the most angst in our lives: changing locations, jobs, spouses, or habits. For example, the battered spouse often stays with her abusive husband because it is easier to remain than to leave. Change is not always comfortable, but sometimes it is necessary.

Sometimes we have to let go

We are held back by the things we hold on to—for example, selfishly seeking fortune or fame—or by the various excuses we make. In Luke 14:15–24, Jesus tells a parable of a man who prepared a great banquet and invited many special guests. But one by one each had an excuse for not attending. One had real estate to check into. Another had bought oxen he had to try out. Another had just got married and so on. So the man opened his great feast to anyone who would make the effort to come. The point, of course, is that we are all invited to God's feast, but many continue to decline the invitation for one reason or another. The result is that we lose out by clinging to things that have no eternal value. The same can be said of the secular world. It important to prioritize wisely, so that we are willing to reach for the more healthy choices in life.

Perhaps we delude ourselves

One thing that prevents us from action is confusion. We rationalize that we are in the process of changing, but we don't really engage in doing it. The great preacher and raconteur of the Second Baptist Church of Houston, pastor Ed Young Sr., tells a story that illustrates this confusion perfectly. In his inimitable Mississippi drawl, pastor Young told of how, while on vacation in Maui, he observed different types of would-be sailors. The first group of "sailors" would go down to the marina on the weekend with their big coolers loaded with drinks and food. They would spend the weekend ensconced in their luxurious boats moored to the slip and then talk to their friends about how they had enjoyed a weekend of sailing. A second set of such sailors would prepare in the same way and enjoy the weekend by cruising around in the marina bay, and they would go on and on about their great, fun weekend of sailing. Still a third crew would get in their boats, untie, and venture out through the marina, cutting loose past the breakwater. They would sail out into the ocean to ride the waves, feel the salt spray in their faces and thrill to the excitement of being on the rolling, open sea.

"So who was actually sailing?" he asked in a pleading voice, with his arms spread wide open. "Only the ones who were willing to cut loose from the ropes that held them back, who took a risk and ventured out into the sea, were actually experiencing sailing. The rest were just fooling themselves."

The correlation to our own lives is obvious. Sometimes the only answer to breaking the status quo is to take a risk, and cut the lines that prevent us from committing fully to "sailing." This applies to athletics, work, family, and certainly to matters of faith. We must be careful in choosing what we hold on to; we need to let go that which holds us back from real joy and contentment, and a more abundant life in all its various aspects. We need to go ahead and step forward to do those things that can help our Life-Teams improve, regardless of our role.

The Shadow Journal

It has been recommended that we keep a journal of our daily transactions. There are a number of people who conscientiously do this. In fact, probably unknowingly, nearly all of us are keeping a "shadow journal." The journal I refer to can be found in our checkbooks and credit card receipts. These instruments will largely describe how a person lives his life. It will indicate how much someone spends on himself or herself as well as on others. It reveals what was used frivolously and how much was spent wisely. It shows the amount that was given away and to whom it was given. It shows what things were valued, and in so doing it can define where the spender's heart is.

Our life account contains more assets than just money, however. When people came out to hear John the Baptist preach, they pleaded, "What shall we do?" And John's reply was, "If you have two tunics, share with one who has none. And if you have food, do the same." Romans 12 tells us that besides using the gifts we have been given, we should "share with those in need and practice hospitality." The point is that there are things we can do beyond our shadow journal, and this may involve things that aren't often recorded in this life. We all have an abundance of something. Sometimes just showing that we care is our gift. It might be to give encouragement. It might involve mentoring another in the right direction. Check the four wheels!

In following the Four-Step System, we will see people develop into more than they were when they started. They will be better players, workers, and friends and so will we. Tony Dungy says the most fulfilling part of mentoring is "seeing how those individuals grow … seeing them come together and function as a unit—with a single purpose in mind—and have some success, and develop lifelong friendships; for me it doesn't get any better than that. Seeing someone becoming more whom God intended them to be—whatever their age—makes it all worthwhile."[10]

Team building is not a new concept at all. It was at the foundation of society from the very beginning of time, starting with the family unit. Unfortunately, our natural human tendency to be more concerned about ourselves than we are about others continues to be a significant factor that works against the team concept. While it is necessary that individuals seek to better themselves, it becomes counterproductive when a personal agenda overrides what is needed for the best functioning of the team, regardless of its composition.

---

10   Dungy, 227.

The proposition set forth here is that each of us possesses the ability to draw out characteristics from within ourselves to aid in team building, and become better role players and potentially more influential in the process.

There are many moments in life in which even the most reluctant must be able to use these skills, and the more we develop them, the better the entire team becomes. We all have roles to fill and these roles will vary between our different groups or teams. We may have one role in our families, another at work, still others in our churches, schools, or organizations. *Regardless of our designated role within a team, we must assist others to play their parts better. Following the patterns we have demonstrated in this study will equip you to be a good team player as you increase your Influence Quotient.*

We have examined some basic leadership skills and how to develop them more fully. However, I believe that building up others on our Life-Teams and being influential when the need arises is more important than raw leadership. None of us can lead all the time. A team with a dozen leaders will be going in too many different directions. Did you ever watch the television show *The View?* That show is a great example of four women going in various directions, doing it quite loudly and generally at the same time. A person who has leadership as his sole aim will generally fail. The system we are talking of here is focused more on influencing others to be their best, which will in turn make the particular Life-Team better for all. And you grow personally in the process. Your goal in life should not be to become the leader in everything you attempt, but to develop attitudes and skills that allow you to be a good team player, who is prepared to lead when there is a need or opportunity.

My emphasis on unity as a vital component for Life-Teams led me to read Tony Evans's book *Oneness Embraced*, which speaks to the need for oneness in the church and particularly addresses the lack of it that still lingers in the church between the races. Evans calls the church "the only authentic cross-racial, cross-cultural and cross-generational basis for oneness in existence ... the only institution on Earth obligated to live under God's authority while enabled to do so through his Spirit."[11]

Dr. Evans adds that unity does not require everyone to be or to act the same: "Unity does not negate the individuality of a person. We have noted this as well by saying that we must have individual missions, but they need to be in harmony with the total (i.e., team) mission." Evans continues, "Unity occurs when we combine our unique differences together, as we reach for a common goal. It is knowing that which we have gathered together for, and are moving toward, is bigger than our own individual preferences."[12]

In his conclusion Evans relies on a sports analogy and uses his favorite one, football. He refers to Super Bowl XXXVI in New Orleans, the first one after the Twin Towers attack of September 2001, during which there was a great sense of oneness prevailing in our country. Four presidents attended that event, and President Bush participated in the coin toss before the game.

An underdog team, the New England Patriots faced off against the favored St. Louis Rams. The Patriots (an ironic and timely name for this event, as it turned out) were not only devoid of superstars; they were missing their main quarterback due to injury. Coach Belichick and the team had, however, put on a tremendous rally

11   Evans, Tony. *Oneness Embraced*. Chicago: Moody, 2011, 45.
12   Ibid., 44.

after the middle of the season to scratch and claw their way into the Super Bowl, and they had survived by holding together as a unit. Therefore, when asked which group Belichick would prefer to introduce as starters, the offense or the defense, he stood firm in insisting that he wanted both of them to get that honor. This was a break from tradition, but it was reluctantly allowed by the NFL commissioner. It has been done that way at each Super Bowl since. During the introductions the teams now run out on the field together as one.

In the game, no one player stood out for the Pats, but the team competed fiercely as a unit from the offense to the defense to the coaching staff. In the end they were able to pull off a great upset by scoring a field goal with only seven seconds remaining in the game. The backup quarterback, who led the offense, refused to accept the traditional automobile that was awarded to the most valuable player. Instead, he turned it over to the team.

Evans notes from this that the church has a goal as well. While that goal involves oneness, he points to an even higher end beyond that watermark achievement: "Unity is simply a way to help reach a higher level. The ultimate goal of the church is to glorify God by reflecting his values among the people, through letting the truth of God be the standard under which all things align."[13]

STUDY

1. Have you ever simply felt stuck in a situation and refused to change because you feared what people might think,

---

13   Ibid., 306–8.

or because it was inconvenient, or would demand more effort? How did that work out?

2. Have you ever been in a situation that you felt needed changing, but the authorities would not budge because they feared change? How did it work out?

3. How has your church/churches responded when people suggested changes in strategy? How flexible should a church be and in what areas should it hold fast under any circumstance?

4. Check into your financial shadow journal over the past six months or year and see what story it reveals about your values.

5. What are you doing in your Life-teams make them more inclusive and unified without being the same?

CHAPTER EIGHT

BETTER LIFE-TEAMS BRING ENDURING, MEANINGFUL RELATIONSHIPS

Life-teams are all about the relationships

One of the things that I have been proud of as I have looked back on my more than fifty years of coaching is the success of my assistant coaches and many players who went into coaching after I had the privilege of coaching them in high school, college, or the NBA. I was head coach for only twelve full years of my more than thirty-seven-year ABA-NBA career. However, I was fortunate to have enough good players to become the nineteenth head coach in NBA history to win 500 games in 1997. But more important than the wins were the relationships and the fact that nearly all of my assistant coaches became head NBA coaches or general managers. Even that may not seem so incredible except that in those twelve years there were eleven men to do this. One general manager was Carroll Dawson, two-time championship GM of the Houston Rockets. The coach of his two championship teams was one of my favorite all-time players and assistant coaches, Rudy Tomjanovich. The other to become a GM was Larry Riley of the Golden State Warriors. More than sixty men whom I had the pleasure to work with as players became coaches, and more than fifty of them became NBA coaches.

That is not to say that I was the chief motivating factor, but many have continued to stay in touch with me for advice or encouragement upon becoming coaches. I always have great pleasure in trying to be of service to them. I may have been a major influence in the case of Larry Harris, one of my sons who became general manager of the Milwaukee Bucks and who is in his third decade of service in the NBA. Of course, I have been equally as proud of my other children, Alex, Stan, Carey Ann, and Dominic, who chose to be successful in other arenas of life, though basketball played a big role in their lives as well.

I think most of my players and coaches would agree I tried to coach in a way that would help them to coach at a high level if they so chose. I told them this often, because my style in coaching was to teach not just the "what" or the "how" but also the "why" of our process. This did give cause for some to say I spent too much time explaining, particularly those who had no inclination to coach, or just didn't care about what they considered inconsequential details. I risked that for the sake of what I considered an essential element of coaching. I know it was a little tough for those who had played for me for several years to hear again what some of the newbies were hearing for the first time. I suffered from the Ricky Ricardo syndrome of *I Love Lucy* fame—I always thought there was some "splainin'" to do.

Can I learn?

As a basketball coach I had to learn to lead. I do not believe that I was born with any special ability to do it. I had been a captain on my college team for two years and had held some elective offices in college, but that was not due to any particular leadership skills. I just happened to be a good player and was able to make enough friends to get elected to a class or club office—and Milligan College was an awfully small college in those days. Then, with no specific instruction or preparation, I was thrust into a role that required me to be a leader when I began coaching basketball in public school at age twenty-two. My first job was at such a small school that I was the coach of all the sports. I was also the assistant coach, trainer, and janitor. At twenty-seven I was head coach of Earlham College in Indiana, and I remained there nine years. During the last seven summers of those years, I was the head coach of pro teams in the Superior League of Puerto Rico as well. We set many records at Earlham College that still exist and won three national championships in Puerto Rico. In addition, my club team, the Bayamon Vaqueros, won a bronze and a silver medal in the World Club Championships in 1973 and 1974. I was also coach of the national team that won a gold medal for Puerto Rico in the Centro-Basket Games of 1974, their first international gold.

By age thirty-seven I was head coach of a professional team in Spain. Then after four years as an assistant coach in the ABA (Utah Stars) and the NBA (Houston Rockets), I was named head coach of the Rockets. In my second year in that position we were playing in the NBA finals against the Boston Celtics. But the irony is that after all that time, I knew very little about being a leader. I was just winging it. I certainly knew nothing that I could have written in a book or even talked about with much certainty.

How did I/we get here?

I suspect many of you older people who may be reading this have gotten to where you are in life in much the same way that I did. If you are like me, you worked your way up or maybe were thrust into a situation in which you were made the leader by default, whether you had leadership skills or not. You probably didn't have a strategic plan or leadership theory. I did not. I just had to play it by ear at the start. It was after the fact that I began to examine how I had reached where I was, and how others had become leaders in their fields. Each of the countless books written on leadership since I started coaching offers some wisdom, but the ideas vary from book to book. If that were not the case, there would be the one definitive book on the subject of leadership and that would be the end of the discussion. However, leadership is an ongoing study due to the dynamism of our society. Yesterday's answers may not work as well today, much less tomorrow. Still, there are fundamentals common to every such endeavor. I think the Four-Step System is logical and practical. It may not make you the leader, but practicing this method will allow you to be influential on your Life-Teams and improve your chances to lead. There were no books like this that I knew of when I started.

As far as relating this to coaching is concerned, I think we are all coaches. Husbands and wives are coaches in the home. CEOs, office managers, and foremen are examples of coaches in the workplace. A coach is a teacher, and we all are called upon to teach at various points in life. I can't tell you specifically how to run your team, your business, or your home without being on-site. Even then, I could guarantee no great results. But I offer some concepts that work for leaders in general and have worked for me.

Align with people of character

Hardcore sports fans will remember that the NBA of the '80s basically belonged to the great Lakers and Celtics teams with some Seventy-

Sixers thrown in between. Because the Bucks were never able to get to the finals, few are aware that the Bucks had the fourth-best record in the NBA in that decade. I was with the team as an aide to Don Nelson from 1983 until I became head coach in 1987. "Nellie" was named NBA Coach of the Year three times in the decade, so he was certainly a coach to be reckoned with. We had a wonderful group of players and exceptional men who passed through Milwaukee in those years. I will mention only a few here, but our success was due to a much larger group of good men willing to play their roles.

For the majority of the period, the team leader was Sidney Moncrief, a shepherd with an excellent but generally low-key style. Few have led any better by example than he did through his consistent work ethic. Concurrently, there were occasions when players like Junior Bridgeman, Brian Winters, Marques Johnson, or Terry Cummings accepted the challenge at game time. Later in the decade, after Moncrief's legs showed the effects of years of yeoman work, players like Jay Humphries, Ricky Pierce, and Jack Sikma stepped to the front. Jay was a tough-minded point guard, and Ricky became one of the best-ever closers in the league. He was a real Mr. Fourth-Quarter Man, a cold-blooded basketball assassin who could score inside, outside, and at the foul line. And in those last years of the decade, one of the best silent leaders, and a great teammate on the court and in the locker room, was our outstanding center Jack Sikma. All these men continued to be successful after their playing days, because they were the ones who were ready to be on point and they learned to be influential in their own way.

Of all the teams that I was associated with in more than thirty years in the NBA, the most intelligent team relative to playing the game was the Milwaukee Bucks. They were incredible in their knowledge and aptitude for the overall game. An amazing number went on to become coaches in the NBA and/or college. From that decade, twenty-four Bucks players became head or assistant coaches in the NBA (eight head coaches) or NCAA Division I (five head coaches). In fact, my 1988–89 team had nine players on the roster who later became NBA coaches. I doubt that any other NBA team ever had more future coaches on it at the same time. While each of the coaches who were Bucks in that decade deserves mention, I will limit the list here to those who have more national familiarity, in order of when they first put on a Bucks jersey: Brian Winters, Quinn Buckner, Sidney Moncrief, Bob Lanier, Dave Cowens, Paul Pressey, Phil Ford, Paul Mokeski, Lorenzo Romar, Mike Dunleavy, Jack Sikma, Scott Skiles, John Lucas, Larry Krystkowiak, and Jay Humphries.

In addition, there were several Bucks members from that era who did not go into coaching but have done extremely well in business or other areas. Among the best known are Junior Bridgeman, Len Elmore, Mike Glenn, Terry Cummings, Tiny Archibald, Kevin Grevey, Harvey Catchings, Steve Mix, Fred Roberts, Marques Johnson, Ricky Pierce and Scott May. It is no wonder the Bucks won a lot of games with that combination of skill and character.

There are different areas in which to lead

In sports there are situations that call for separate styles of leadership. For example, one may be the actual leader on the court for most of the game, while there can be a "closer" type who has the ability to take over a game at crunch time. Another may be the leader in the locker room, one who keeps order and discipline when things start unraveling due to a losing situation. He may be one who intervenes when teammates are having personality clashes. He is often called the "spiritual" leader.

Yet another, often-unheralded leader may be one who stimulates the team to work harder because of his attitude and relentless approach in practice. He motivates others to play hard, even when they don't want to do it that day. Though unsung, this latter type is an important factor on any team or in any workplace. He may be called the "heart of the team." Joakim Noah of the Chicago Bulls is one of those who typify the latter. Early in his career, his infectious work ethic in practice helped the Bulls become a play-off team when preseason polls ignored them. By his fourth season, along with Derrick Rose and Luol Deng, the Bulls had become one of the NBA's premier teams.

Quite obviously, a certain measure of leadership is of the essence to a point guard's success in basketball and to being "on point" in life. When one looks at the outstanding teams of any era, it is easy to identify the leadership that was instrumental to their success. The history of the great champions in the NBA is filled with names of great players who stepped to the fore at either critical or propitious times. Some were point guards like Bob Cousy, Magic Johnson and Isaiah Thomas, Tony Parker and Jason Kidd. Some played positions other than point guard, such as Bill Russell, Jerry West, Elgin Baylor, Larry Bird, Michael Jordan, Kareem Abdul-Jabbar, Joe Dumars, Tim Duncan, Manu Ginobili, Dwyane Wade, Dirk Nowitzki, LeBron James, and many more. Some among these took over control principally at one end of the court, as did Russell on defense. Some were coaches—Red Auerbach, Chuck Daly, Phil Jackson, Gregg Popovich, and Red Holzman, to name a few notables. Each did what he could do according to his gift or gifts to answer the call to leadership. But none could have had the success they had without lesser-known players or assistant coaches who were the underpinning and who were able to be of great influence in the outcomes. It is indisputable that more than 80 percent of NBA players are role players. The stars cannot possibly win without those players' contributions. They are influential, and that has great value.

It is the most unique of people who can be a leader for all occasions, and that is why there must be good role players who are ready to step to the point. Every good team or organization needs these people—those with the ability and readiness to answer the call when necessary, but willing to be good team players until their opportunity beckons. We must all be ready to be one of those people who can be counted to be on point when no one else is willing or able to serve. It behooves all of us to enhance our Life-Team skills in order to do that. Yes, we can learn how to become influential people and many will develop into leaders in the process on one or more of their Life-Teams.

MAXWELL'S VARIOUS LEVELS OF LEADERSHIP

As we work to improve our Influence Quotient, I want to paraphrase from a list of leadership levels written by John C. Maxwell and then expand on them with some personal observations. Maxwell is one of the giants among leadership gurus, and he presents a tremendous analysis on the subject in *Developing the Leader Within You*, one of his many titles on leadership. In Maxwell's thinking there are five levels of leadership to consider: position, permission, production, people development, and personhood.[14]

Leaders by position

As we consider this list, we recognize that parents, coaches and owners of businesses in general are among those who are automatically placed in leadership by position. Nonetheless, it is not uncommon at

---

14   Maxwell, John C. *Developing the Leader Within You.* Nashville: Nelson, 1993, 5–10 .

all these days for this category of leader to lose effectiveness, possibly even early on. Most parents, if they make any effort at all, can maintain their lead status through the preadolescent years. However, any parent who has survived raising children through the teenage years can verify that advancing beyond basic positional leadership can be severely tested. In sports, professional head coaches have difficulty surviving beyond three years with the same franchise. For that reason even the most successful coaches have been in charge of multiple teams over the course of their careers. And corporate bosses understand from the start that, unless they are also the owner of the operation, their tenure depends on their continued effectiveness. In light of the acknowledged difficulty of maintaining control of the reins, Tony Dungy asserts that the best way to gain and maintain a following in your initial position is to let people know your number-one priority is to help them. And there is no better way to show that than by demonstrating your desire to serve.[15]

Leaders by permission

These may have worked their way up from the previous starting point and moved from being leaders by position to this next level. This needs to happen in a healthy family situation, of course. That is, once children become more aware of who their parents are as people, they will decide whether to accept their parents' lead or not, depending on whether adequate trust has been earned. Whether in the home or workplace, however, those who start by being positional leaders will have to earn the respect of their followers if they want to continue to be influential.

15 Dungy, 212.

In time, the followers will decide if they like the leadership style and whether they want to continue to follow. This can happen when people join an organization and must follow existing leaders but later will choose whether to remain members or not, depending on the level of trust their leaders have earned. A caring relationship must develop and grow for the alliance to continue. If leaders—parents, coaches, or bosses—fail to achieve such a relationship, their leadership is unlikely to continue. Their followers will reject their leadership by ignoring their counsel or by leaving. As noted in our introduction, becoming a successful point person requires ongoing proof of concern for followers, but improvement and growth must develop as well.

Production leadership

This can develop from the permission level as a successful relationship continues to grow over time, but it may not have a long shelf life. We tend to be results-oriented by nature. People in general want to see tangible positive results on a continuing basis. Even loving families are not exempt from this, and certainly all other connections will be effectiveness-oriented or results-oriented. This is true whether a sports team, a business, a charity, or a church is involved. Relationships often break down when the "team" is not productive, relative to its understood purpose, even when adequate caring exists. "Business is business" is given as the reason for tough-love action in every arena. And it's never good business that they reference. There needs to be a continuation and a sharing of glory that only a successful operation can produce. If stagnation occurs, the fervor of the following will gradually wane and people will move on to something else.

For example, NBA players say they want to play the game as long as it is fun and talk about what a great time they are having with the team's great "chemistry" as long as things are going smoothly. Once that momentum is lost, and particularly when it becomes apparent that expected goals will not be met, leadership—the coach, the point guard, the best player, the GM, or even the owner—usually begins to lose followers. The same is true of other systems and the results can be devastating. Red ink on the bottom line of the company will result in cutbacks, or worse yet, the closure of the company. Churches and volunteer organizations are far from exempt. Dissatisfied people will break away in groups to join other entities, or will split off to start their own organization, business or church. More likely, the leadership will be replaced before the worst of these circumstances occurs.

Complacency must never set in with the leadership. Regardless of the length of the operation's profitability, leadership stands to lose control if it loses momentum. In pro sports it is called "losing the team." Maintaining the status quo is not acceptable in a competitive situation. Just like investors, clients want to see growth in their investments. And people like to see growth in themselves as well. Leadership must accept that followers are going to be largely those who wonder what is in it for them. In the end, they may talk of what a "great person the leader was, but …"

People development

In the fourth phase, those who have been followers in a successful endeavor may come to the point where they want to surpass the existing leadership and go to the next level themselves. This phase easily relates to loving families in which those who had a successful family experience while growing up will view becoming parents themselves as a natural progression. Those who lacked a positive childhood are more inclined to hesitate before choosing this path.

Businesses and virtually all other entities produce people who want to assume leadership roles. The more aggressive and motivated people will not be satisfied to remain assistants or vice presidents. Those who have followed a leader who has successfully led them from position to permission to production levels and on to the people development level often want to continue in the path of the point person with whom they have been working. The confident leader at this level works constantly to develop this aspiration in those who are in his charge.

While some leaders fear that those following them will take their jobs, the most effective ones know that if their followers improve, the entire operation advances as well. When everyone on the team is of the same mind, the leader promotes the effectiveness of his lieutenants to others as they develop. In the best situations, advancement is a natural and positive outcome rather than a threat to the leader. Loyalty readily develops in the ranks, and successful efforts are rewarded as everyone grows.

Personhood level

Finally, some leaders are able to transcend the high plateau in leadership, represented by the fourth of Maxwell's five levels, and move on to the ultimate personhood level. On this plane, those who have replace a retired leader, or who have become leaders of other departments or entities, develop loyalty and respect for the methods of their mentor. They copy many of the strategies and some of the personal characteristics of their former leader, who may continue as a consultant, and take great joy in the successes of those with whom he has been associated. This, of course, is the ultimate in the development of Life-Teams. Good environments build up trust and loyalties so meaningful relationships are established. Children want to be like their parents; former players want to coach as their coaches did; and operate in a manner similar to their mentor-manager.

Developing leadership is a journey in which we learn as we go. Very few are natural-born leaders, so do not fret or give in. Observe, study, and prepare. There are levels of leadership, and each requires concern for the individual if the leader wants to be influential. Effective leaders strive to get to the fourth and fifth levels of effectiveness for maximum fulfillment. The combinations of responses and characteristics described in our Four-Step System provide the means to create an environment in which healthy relationships can flourish.

Relationships are in our DNA

Proof of our desire for relationships is demonstrated by our involvement in family life, fraternities, churches, clubs, and even gangs. In Heaven, God, the Son, and the Spirit, are always surrounded by a host of angels. God created human beings with the idea of forging a relationship with us. He has instituted the family unit as the primary relational element on Earth to fulfill our innate desire for companionship, but he hopes we will want more. When we are at our highest or our lowest, whether joyful or in utmost need, we tend to want to find someone to share or to help us in that moment. We seek to share with a loved one or friend. Sometimes, anyone we can find will do. Why do we adore pets? To be watchdogs? Really! How many of our pets would actually attack anyone? It's all about relationships, and good leaders foster that in their groups. Good Life-Teams foster strong associations. Above all, God wants us to cultivate the kind of relationships that lead to a closer one with him.

I hope I have made the case that successful Life-Teams can best be developed through a systematic step-by-step process. You can more easily forge positive relationships in a family or organization by going through the Four-Step System we have defined. You cannot expect to demonstrate important external characteristics of a good relationship unless you first develop the necessary internal qualities. The logical sequence of steps presented here can lead to successful relationships that begin now and are eternal.

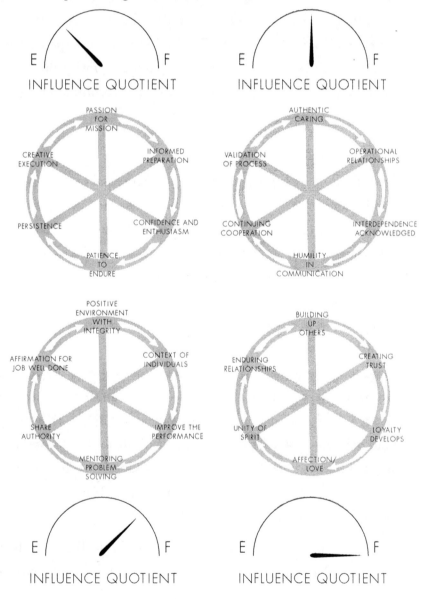

STUDY

1. Think of a leader in some area of your life—parent, teacher, boss, coach, etc.—who has been a favorite of yours. Examine what stage that leader reached as you consider Maxwell's list of the Five Levels of Leadership.

2. Give a specific example to support your opinion. In what way(s) will you try to duplicate that person's style of influencing?

3. Have you had a leader fail to live up to what you expected? In that case, describe where he or she got stuck on the ladder.

4. What do you make of the statement, "We are all coaches?"

5. Have you had clear opportunities to lead in your life? If so, what would you describe as your style? Will you seek to continue in that pattern, or will you try to modify it? In either case, ask yourself, why?

AFTERWORD

The Four Step Program

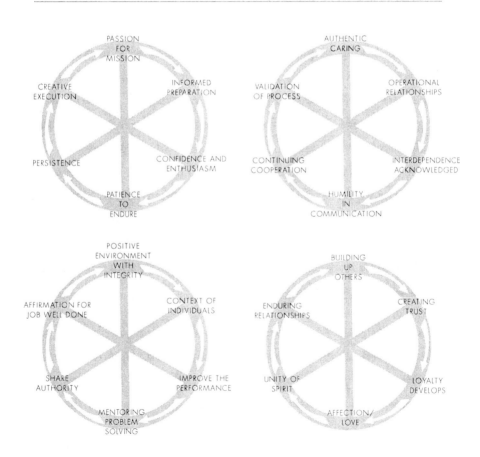

PASSION FOR MISSION
INFORMED PREPARATION
CREATIVE EXECUTION
PERSISTENCE
CONFIDENCE AND ENTHUSIASM
PATIENCE TO ENDURE

AUTHENTIC CARING
OPERATIONAL RELATIONSHIPS
VALIDATION OF PROCESS
CONTINUING COOPERATION
INTERDEPENDENCE ACKNOWLEDGED
HUMILITY IN COMMUNICATION

POSITIVE ENVIRONMENT WITH INTEGRITY
AFFIRMATION FOR JOB WELL DONE
CONTEXT OF INDIVIDUALS
SHARE AUTHORITY
IMPROVE THE PERFORMANCE
MENTORING PROBLEM SOLVING

BUILDING UP OTHERS
ENDURING RELATIONSHIPS
CREATING TRUST
UNITY OF SPIRIT
LOYALTY DEVELOPS
AFFECTION/ LOVE

Dear reader, please review the diagrams of our Four-Step System on the previous page and read the selected scriptures below as a quick reminder of the validity of these concepts. The key words are in italics and at times I have inserted a similar word that we have used in our discussion in the book. It may be a good thing to photocopy this page or tear it out as a reminder of the value of building up your own Influence Quotient. Blessings to you in all you do. May your Life-Teams all be blessed as well, and may you be a blessing to others. (All scriptures in this book are quoted from the New International Version: Grand Rapids, MI: Zondervan, 2005.)

Romans 12:6–13: "We have different gifts, according to the grace given us. If a man's gift is prophesying, let him use it in proportion to his faith. If it is serving, let him *serve*; if it is teaching, let him *teach*; (mentor) if it is encouraging, let him *encourage*; if it is contributing to the needs of others, let him *give* generously; if it is leadership (influence), let him *govern* diligently; if it is showing mercy, let him do it cheerfully. Love must be sincere. Hate what is evil; cling to what is good. Be devoted to one another in *brotherly love*. Honor one another above yourselves (humility). Never be lacking in zeal, but keep your spiritual fervor (enthusiasm), serving the Lord. Be *joyful* in hope, *patient* in affliction, faithful in prayer. *Share* with God's people who are in need. Practice hospitality.

Colossians 3:12–14: "Therefore, as God's chosen people, holy and dearly loved, clothe yourselves with *compassion, kindness, humility, gentleness and patience*. Bear with each other and *forgive whatever grievances* you may have against one another. Forgive as the Lord forgave you. And over all these virtues put on *love, which binds them all together in perfect unity*.

1 Thessalonians 5:11–12: "Therefore *encourage* one another and *build each other up*, just as in fact you are doing. Now we ask you, brothers, *to respect those who work hard among you* (acknowledge), who are over you in the Lord and who admonish you.

1 Thessalonians 5:16–18: "*Be joyful* always; pray continually; *give thanks* in all circumstances, *for this is God's will* for you in Christ Jesus."

PERSONAL PROGRAM

1. Develop your own road map by designing a wheel or wheels (some internal, some external aspects) that you follow for one month to see how your "team/s" respond.

2. Review your mission, select your goals, and write down the personalized points you will need to refine to accomplish it.

3. For this to work you must commit it to paper and review the diagram of your program every day.

4. Ideally, you should create a short journal, relative to your daily ups and downs.

5. At the end of a month, see if you have changed in any way, or if perhaps others around you have changed.

BIBLIOGRAPHY

Maxwell, John C. *Developing the Leader Within You.*
Nashville: Thomas Nelson Publishers, 1993.

Pellerin, Charles J. *How NASA Builds Teams.*
Hoboken, NJ: John Wiley and Sons, 2009.

Maxwell, John C. *The 21 Irrefutable Laws of Leadership.*
Nashville: Thomas Nelson, 1998.

Buford, Bob. *Game Plan.* Grand Rapids:
Zondervan Publishing Co., 1997.

———. *Halftime.* Grand Rapids: Zondervan Publishing Co., 1994.

Ortberg, John. *When the Game Is Over It All Goes Back
in the Box.* Grand Rapids: Zondervan, 2007.

Yancey, Philip. *The Jesus I Never Knew.* Grand
Rapids: Zondervan, 1995.

Evans, Tony. *Oneness Embraced.* Chicago: Moody, 2011.

———. *Kingdom Man.* Carol Stream, IL: Tyndale House, 2012.

Dungy, Tony. *The Mentor Leader*. Carol Stream, IL: Tyndale House, 2010.

Tutu, Bishop Desmond. *Believe*. Boulder, CO: Philips, 2007.

Peter Vescey. "Teammates recall Lucas' eternal friendship". *New York Post*, Nov. 2, 2010.

Moore, David. "Why Pats sizzle, 'Boys fizzle? NE's Kraft eliminates meddle man". *Dallas Morning News*, Feb. 7, 2012.

ABOUT DEL HARRIS

ONPOINTLIFETEAM@GMAIL.COM

WWW.ONPOINTLIFETEAM.COM

Education History

- Milligan College (1959), A.B. Religion, Cum Laude

- Indiana University (1965), M.A.T., History

- Bilingual, Spanish.

Coaching Accomplishments—NBA

- NBA Coach of the Year, 1995.

- 19th head coach to win 500 NBA games in 1997.

- Listed in *NBA Register* under All Time Great Coaches.

- 542 NBA victories in only 12 full seasons as a head coach; 11 made the playoffs.

International Coaching Experience

- **An American pioneer in international basketball (FIBA).**

- Articles and books on all phases of basketball and lectured around the world on basketball for over 40 years.

- **Coached 5 different countries' national teams**—winning 2 gold, 1 silver and 3 bronze medals. Coached in two World Championships and one Olympics.

- **2004—Olympics in Athens.** Head Coach of National Team of China. Finished in top 8, winning greatest game in Chinese history in beating defending world champion, Serbia, to get into the medal round.

Assistant Coaching Highlights

- Selected best assistant in league by NBA.com GM poll three times and third twice, in his last five years, including first in each of his last two years in Dallas.

- Three coaches he worked for made Coach of the Year during his time with them.

- Mentor to beginning coaches Avery Johnson and Vinny Del Negro.

- 202 NBA playoff games on bench as head or assistant coach.

College Coaching Highlights

- Winningest coach in Earlham College history.
- Coach of Year various times.
- Indiana Basketball Hall of Fame.
- NAIA Basketball Hall of Fame.

Publications

- *Winning Defense*—McGraw-Hill, 1994, 1995.

- *Playing the Game*—Word Pub. Co., 1984.

- *Basketball's Zone Offenses*—Prentice Hall, 1975.

- *Multiple Defenses for Winning Basketball*—Prentice-Hall, 1971.

- *Big Bang of Basketball, a history of early Indiana basketball,* wrote the foreword, 2010.

- *NBA Coaches Instructional Book,* 2008. Wrote final chapter on game-ending situations.

- Various coaching magazine and publication contributions.

- Writings have been translated into five different languages.

Community Service/Philanthropic Endeavors

- Del and Ann Harris Foundation since 2002—has donated many scholarships and contributed to missions and other worthy causes.

- Honorary Board of Coaches of Influence (COIN), Los Angeles, CA.

- Honorary Board, Elevate Your Game, inner city program, Dallas, TX.

- President's Council, Urban Alternative, Dallas/National inner city education program.

- Philanthropy Award, Wernle Children's Home, Richmond, IN, 2012.

Other Endeavors

- Adjunct Professor, Dallas Christian College 2011-12.

- Bilingual—Analyst for Dallas Mavericks home games, Fox Spanish Network, 2010-current; Analyst on ESPN Spanish Radio for 1996 NBA finals.

- MIT Sloan Conference on Metrics in Sports, panelist—Boston, 2010.

- SAG-AFTRA member, having done various TV and movie roles including his own radio and TV shows, the movie "Space Jam," sitcoms such as "Diagnosis Murder," "In the House," and others.

- Ordained minister, Christian Church, 1958.

- Public Speaker—hundreds of public speaking appearances.

How can you use this book?

MOTIVATE

EDUCATE

THANK

INSPIRE

PROMOTE

CONNECT

Why have a custom version of *On Point*?

- Build personal bonds with customers, prospects, employees, donors, and key constituencies
- Develop a long-lasting reminder of your event, milestone, or celebration
- Provide a keepsake that inspires change in behavior and change in lives
- Deliver the ultimate "thank you" gift that remains on coffee tables and bookshelves
- Generate the "wow" factor

Books are thoughtful gifts that provide a genuine sentiment that other promotional items cannot express. They promote employee discussions and interaction, reinforce an event's meaning or location, and they make a lasting impression. Use your book to say "Thank You" and show people that you care. *On Point* is designed for church small group studies with study questions after each chapter.

CPSIA information can be obtained at www.ICGtesting.com
Printed in the USA
LVOW10s0929230114

370641LV00004B/4/P